To my mother
Nancy Veronica Ahern

ABOUT THE AUTHOR

John was born in Queensland, Australia, and grew up in Redcliffe where he roamed the beaches and played backyard cricket with his mates. His career spanned from mowing lawns and packing groceries to get through university to being the global head of Real Estate and Acquisitions for a public listed travel company.

In between serious bouts of work, he has travelled through over eighty countries and been shot at, poisoned, tear-gassed, robbed at gunpoint and locked up in an African jail. He has also stowed away in a Colombian cargo plane, ridden across countries on the back of trucks and the roofs of buses, flown in an ultralight over the Zambezi, and been a passenger in two train derailments.

He now lives with his wife and two children in the comparative safety of the Currumbin Valley on Australia's Gold Coast. He considers it their base camp for new adventures.

www.johnahern.co
@johnahernoz

CONTENTS

ON THE
ROAD
...WITH KIDS

Lofoten Island

Geiranger

Copenhagen

START/END

London

Amsterdam

Luxembourg

Paris

Munic

Loire Valley

Santiago de Compostela

Bilbao

Bl

Turin

Venice

Porto

Andorra

Nice

Madrid

Lisbon

Barcelona

Ri

Lagos

Nap

Gibraltar

Tangier

Casablanca

Fes

Marrakech

Agadir

Sidi Ifni

Erg Chebbi

Lapland
Rovaniemi
Helsinki
Tallin
Riga
Warsaw
Kraków
Budapest
Belgrade
Dubrovnik
Sofia
Istanbul
Bari
Meteora
Igoumenitsa
Gallipoli
Göreme
Nemrut Dagi
Kas

ROUTE MAP

Travel is at its most rewarding when it ceases to be about realising a destination and becomes indistinguishable from living your life.
Paul Theroux

There is nothing like returning to a place that remains unchanged to find the ways in which you yourself have changed.
Nelson Mandela

1

LIVING BETWEEN
THE LINES

I have always liked plane travel at night. It's as if I am in a dark, peaceful bubble being soothed by the gentle throb of the engine and the repetitive hum of the air conditioning. No one can bother me. Except for tonight. Tonight I had the seat from hell.

I was on the aisle in the centre row of four. A small noisy girl was next to me, then her mother, then a smaller louder boy. The children were bouncing on the chairs and over the harried woman, flicking lights on and off, wailing, and slapping over juice cups as though they were bowling pins. The mother had clearly lost control.

Every now and then the little girl froze and gave me a demonic stare. I burrowed deeper into my blanket hoping to be too inanimate to be of interest. Closing my eyes I wished myself back to my high-flying corporate days when I sometimes flew business class. Flat beds; fine wines; no plastic forks; movies of choice. And best of all... no kids!

As though telepathic, an air hostess soon glided down the aisle, winked conspiratorially and offered me a row of three empty seats away from the adjoining circus. I hesitated for an appropriate second, then launched across the aisle as though shot from an ejector seat.

When my wife, Mandy, distracted by another of our kids' drink spills, finally noticed my absence, she looked at me as though I had just taken the last chopper out of a hot zone.

Mandy and I took turns in the three-seat row during the flight, allowing me space to think about what lay ahead. There were a lot of unknowns to consider. I may have been strapped in by the seatbelts but couldn't restrain my thoughts from running off in anticipation. They all focused on the seven-berth motor home waiting for us in the Netherlands. Months earlier, we'd zapped off 14,000 euros to buy it over the internet. I was slightly concerned we had been sucked into an internet scam, but the image of this wonderful craft had been seared into my mind for months, even dreamt about for years, and had recently transformed into a magical starship that promised to provide our travelling family with nirvana for the next year.

Consequently, two days later, on a grey Tuesday morning in August, on the way to view this new motor home, I was so excited I was quivering more than a wet puppy in a cold wind. The dream was about to come true.

Donna, an eccentric Dutch American who bought and sold used motor homes for a living, chatted away about her cats while weaving her little red Fiat from lane to lane down the motorway out of Utrecht. As her car could only carry one passenger, Mandy and the kids had remained back at the hotel, mainly because I had begged and pleaded with Mandy to be the first to drive the machine. Donna soon pulled off the highway and the car bounced down a narrow dirt path, stopping behind a dilapidated old farmhouse and windmill.

'It's in here, John.' She pointed to the windmill. It seemed a very strange place for a professional operation to store motor homes.

Donna jumped out of her car and wrenched back the windmill's big timber doors in a surprising show of strength. 'Look. Look at it!' she cried.

I peered beyond the doors and felt an instant gush of relief. Inside the shed were rows of renovated gleaming antique cars. Donna obviously had a passion for autos and was just the right person, I thought, to have cared for our new home during the past few months since we'd bought it. I squinted further into the dark recesses of the shed, eager for the first view of the motor home, as though on a blind date. Donna flicked a switch, the lights blinked and a dark shape slowly came into focus.

I gaped in silence, frozen to the ground. This first sight of our motor home was supposed to be a moment of exultation, of trumpets blaring 'Hallelujah', declaring a life-reclaiming event was about to begin. Instead I stared in complete and utter devastation.

In the rear corner of the shed sat a big white box with faded red racing stripes down the side. The engine bonnet was open, with cables attached to various parts as though it were on life support. The 'thing' was covered in a thick film of dust. It sat there discarded, disowned and decrepit, in teasing contrast to the sparkling antiques surrounding it.

'We've had some problems getting it started,' Donna said.

'Uh huh,' was my reply.

Mandy and I had gambled everything for this shit heap. We had no jobs, no income and had just torn a hole in our savings. Our car was sold, the house rented, probably to the Manson family. All our beloved possessions were in a storage shed gathering cobwebs. We were about to launch into a world without TV, internet, telephones, friends, family, toys or schooling for the kids. We had an old laptop with some children's DVDs, one small backpack of clothes each and no idea where we were going or for how long. And I was about to sleep, eat, pee and shower together with my wife and our two kids for a year in this rolling box smaller than our bedroom. I stared long and hard at the motor home, wondering again how I had got here.

It all began on Christmas Day the year before. My brother-in-law Terry and I had been playing a swashbuckling game of table tennis, progressively hitting the balls harder as we smashed our way around; two male egos in our own gladiatorial ping-pong arena. With two points to win, I launched across the table wildly. Swinging the bat in a long arc, pain ripped into my back as though a sniper had shot me with a hot bullet. In noiseless slow motion I landed on the ground. For long seconds I lay there staring at the sky, waiting, blinking.

'Get up, ya wimp!' came the call from across the net.

I moved and cried out in pain. I immediately thought I had burst a disc, but I was wrong. I had burst two discs, the lower two.

This was the first in a series of shock strikes that would create the revolutionary period I would later refer to as when my back went 'snap' and my career went 'poof'.

I was mostly bedridden for the next two weeks, sucking on Valium pills like they were sugar-coated lollies. The drugs worked on my back but could not dull my whirring brain. I insisted on working, literally flat out, making calls to the office from my bed and whacking away on the laptop day and night. I was on the executive team for a global public listed company, and had been negotiating to buy another company in India for the past year. It had become my own personal mission that I lived and breathed.

Unfortunately my kids didn't understand the gravity of the situation. They kept surging into my bedroom, curious and entertained by the sight of their dad, horizontal and at home during the day.

My four-year-old daughter Jaimie, as usual, led the charge one sunny morning, her blonde hair falling down over her blue eyes and freckles. She stood, smiling in her giraffe pyjamas with a hopeful glint in her eye, the spokesperson for every plot she and her two-year-old brother Callum hatched. He was smaller, with his grandmother's olive skin and a mop of brown hair, and stood loyally next to her in red Spider-Man pyjamas waiting for my attention. They reminded me of C-3PO and R2-D2, the taller, chattier one always blaming the littler one who couldn't speak properly for anything that went wrong.

'Do you want to play dolly with us... pleeease?' Jaimie pleaded, handing me her unattractive doll.

I held 'Scary Dolly', as she was affectionately known, up in front of my laptop. 'Oh, I can't, kiddies. I have to work.' Scary Dolly and her two pyjama-clad sidekicks would have to wait.

'Aw! Can you sing "Barbie Girl" with us?'

That was one of my specialties. 'Nup. Sorry. Later.'

Their faces dropped and they soon scurried off, but my eyes followed them, a little thought drifting like a ghost behind them.

I started replaying the past few days and nights. I'd watched Mandy pick the kids up and put them to bed while I stood by like a broken appendage. When would I be able to hold them? And how could I keep a job if I couldn't sit upright? My work? Shit, my work! What was I doing? I had no time for these distractions. I turned back to my computer, but soon floated further off into weird thought-bubbles of acute clarity, losing hours staring at the ceiling, thinking.

Pop! My work sucked. Well, more so the people, not the actual work. I had buried this knowledge for some time, but the unusual cocktail of excessive spare time, a comfy big bed and Valium pills had burst the thought wide open. An influx of new people had created a pervading 'me' culture at work. Trust and loyalty were eroding. Redundancies were happening for the first time. I had revelled in the company for over a decade and I wasn't averse to change but not like this.

Weeks later I popped painkillers to attend an important board meeting to summarise the Indian deal. After so much isolated time in bed, my brain was whirring with conflicting thoughts and I entered the boardroom in a rather skittish frame of mind. The chairman was a legend of the corporate scene who delivered questions rapid fire and expected precise answers.

I was soon given the floor but was immediately cut off by one of my team members who took over the presentation. I was gobsmacked, but decided a confrontation in front of the board would not be good. Instead I eased back into my chair and tried to look unflustered.

The presentation started with 'As John was not available...' confirming the 'me' games I had avoided so well were now upon me. I don't know if it was the Valium or my sudden wish to be transported from the situation, but my mind drifted off to memories of a fellow I'd contracted to paint my house years earlier. I remembered he was always up on the roof, which was odd given I wasn't getting the roof painted.

'Hey Johnno!' he screamed one afternoon. 'Can't you see it, man?'

'See what?' I jumped, looking around for a snake.

'The lines!' the mad painter yelled. 'You're living between the lines, man!'

Standing in my shiny polyester grey suit, the 25-year-old me yelled upwards, 'What are you talking about, man?' This was back when it was cool to call everyone 'man'.

'The fucking lines, man! They're trying to box us in! Everywhere you go, there are lines. This block of land,' he waved his paintbrush. 'Fences! Driving down the road... fucking lanes. Queuing at the bank! Swim between the flags. They're trying to cage us in, man!'

I laughed. 'Don't worry, man. It won't happen to me.'

'Ha! You're already trapped, you poor bastard!' he screeched. 'You know it! Hopping to the beat. Playing the games. Get out. Escape… while you can!'

Was that even possible? It occurred to me that this boardroom world had played a large part in snuffing out the adventure in my existence. Riding on the rooftops of buses in Africa, or stowing away on a Colombian cargo plane over the Amazon, felt like dreams rather than memories. I heard my name and snapped back to attention, then realised it was only being used in the context of me not being available the last few weeks. I chuckled, but it wasn't a happy chuckle. What folly, I thought. Here I was, barely able to sit up, and playing around me was a game of ego. My biggest worry over the past month had not been that I couldn't carry my kids to bed but rather that some business in India might not get purchased.

There was something awfully wrong with my priorities and, right then, the stranger I had become finally struck me. I was dragging myself to meetings at the expense of my health and ignoring my family at the same time. My career had become my defining priority. My social life was my work life. Adventure was a bygone concept. The mad painter was right. I had to escape.

'Anything else to add, John… from your perspective?' The pointed question jolted me out of my delirious state. All the important faces wheeled around at me like gun turrets. I stared back down their barrels taking in each one of them. I saw mentors, good guys and sociopaths.

The seconds ticked away as they waited for my reply. My statement needed to be witty, detailed, professional and balanced. I had to brilliantly retake control.

But I no longer wanted to play. It suddenly all seemed so silly.

My leg was jiggling under the table. It was a moment of discovery that I will never forget. It was the moment, for my working world, that I no longer gave a fuck.

I didn't even get up. I just took a deep breath, hoisted the white flag and said, 'Nope.'

In the taxi home I became marginally psychotic, slapping myself on the forehead for my stupidity. Then I laughed, crazy like a demon. Then reality knocked again. I may have wanted to stick my middle finger in the air towards the working world, but I didn't have that luxury. I was a husband and a father of two. I was the current breadwinner. We had a mortgage and responsibilities. My 'nope' was a blip. It had to be.

With the acceptance that career and parenthood had captured my life, I trudged back into the house and slumped down on the couch feeling like I may as well have sawn off my own testes and hung them in the company trophy cabinet. The house was in darkness, the kids were in bed. It was a familiar scene: me arriving home late, a meal sitting on the kitchen bench with plastic covering it, waiting to be reheated.

Mandy bounced down the stairs, keen to talk to someone over the age of four. I filled her in on my mad moment of surrender and started discussing my unavoidable fight-back before being interrupted by the kids' yells about a spider in their room. Mandy went to investigate, leaving me on the couch thinking.

It was becoming a dangerous pastime, this thinking. I knew that something had broken in me that day. And I knew I should be the one smashing that giant crab spider; killing poisonous critters was one of my key roles in the family. And yet my back meant I couldn't even do that. What was left?

Mandy returned to find me staring at her.

'What's life really about?' I punched my hands together. 'Living it!' I shouted before she could reply. 'This back thing. It's a wake-up call! Life can be snatched away in a nanosecond! Why does it have to take a massive tragedy in people's lives before they stop and think, shit, am I really enjoying this?' I paused to collect my thoughts. 'What if I died tomorrow? Was hit by a bus? What if I was diagnosed with cancer and given a few months to live?'

She raised her eyebrows waiting for the answer.

I asked her to think of a fantasy, a dream, maybe a great purpose... and then imagine actually doing it. Tapping into something that makes you so excited your heart pumps and you gasp for breath. 'That's what life is about!'

She was as confused by this dramatic enthusiasm as she had been with my previous despairing self. 'Go on,' she said, leaning forward. 'I'm listening.'

'Well, we haven't done anything outrageous in ages,' I continued. 'We can't just meander along collecting more TVs and end up at the Pearly Gates with a bunch of assets, "if onlys" and "what ifs"! So let's do it!'

'Do what?'

Now all my dangerous thinking converged on one point. 'Well... you know I've always said that one of my dreams was to hoot around Europe in an old orange VW camper.'

'Bit late,' she laughed, holding up a dirty nappy as though it were a visual aid. 'That was when you were twenty-two.'

I chose to ignore this ageist remark. 'But it doesn't have to be too late. They're talking about redundancies at work. If it happened to me, we could just take the payout and go!'

'Oh rubbish! They won't sack you. And anyway, if they did, we'd need that money to survive on.'

'Yes, and that would be the responsible thing to do. But... and this is just a thought,' I paused for effect. 'What about if we just say fuck it and go?'

Mandy was a traveller from way back. Despite being only five foot two with a bob of brown hair, she had been a formidable tour guide across Russia and Egypt, herding tourists around like stray cats and dealing with everything from her driver's rampant sexual exploits among the punters, to talking down suicide attempts. It was her sharp wit and acute, searching intelligence that had always both attracted and challenged me. Not to mention her blonde surfie look when we first got together. We had once regularly sipped wine and babbled away into the wee hours about wandering the world, but these dreams had been sealed into a locked closet since we became parents.

Mandy had turned away from her corporate career some years earlier to chase her passion for writing. It was a joint decision but the advent of kids and Mandy's desire to be at home with them while juggling her writing had slowly eroded our egalitarianism. To say we had drifted apart was a stretch, but we both knew we could enter that slippery road at any time.

'OK. I like those four words. Fuck it and go. So how?'

I calculated how much the redundancy payment would be. 'Let's buy a camper and do it. What's the point in waiting till we're retired to live our dreams? We may not be around or physically able to then anyway.'

'And what about the kids?'

'Come on. You're thinking between the lines, man. We get like a Winnebagoey thingy, a big one. Six berth. Kitchen on board. Toilet, shower, TV, bikes strapped on the back. The works!'

I could hear her mind ticking. She'd spent the past two months nursing me, driving me everywhere, and dealing with my frustrations and moods. This was not a sane suggestion. She got up and walked across the room and out onto the deck. I was waiting for all the negatives. After all, she hadn't had the benefit of bedridden weeks of accumulated thinking time.

'We've always talked about heading off again,' I called and then added dramatically, 'travel is like air to us. We're suffocating without it!'

She eventually returned and stood in front of me. 'No TV,' she said.

I was confused.

'We're not having a TV in my camper.'

I scanned her face and realised she was beaming. 'Yes!' I punched the air.

'One more thing,' she said.

'Yeah. What? Anything.'

'Why did you just call me man?'

We had agreed to take the plunge but our logical brains kept us frozen in inaction. It was too big a risk, too much change. Then a week later, I was summoned to another meeting. This time there was just the CEO and one other manager, both nervous and stumbling through words as though a bee had stung their tongues. After some minutes of verbal Twister the CEO eventually straightened and said, 'We're going to have to make you redundant.'

Rejoice! It was exactly what I wanted; what Mandy and I had plotted. We could start reclaiming our life!

Then I thought maybe it was a joke. Surely the past ten years of hard work I'd given the company meant something? I sat there disbelieving. Like a jilted lover, I suddenly wanted no part in this divorce. I rationalised that I had given up the moment I said 'nope' in the boardroom a week earlier, but yet the rejection sucked the wind out of me. I eventually wandered away from the meeting, realising that there was no longer any 'me' in their corporate 'we'.

I returned to my desk later to find police tape on the floor in the shape of a murder victim, a not-so-subtle staff protest against people being 'executed' in the redundancy process. I smiled at that and walked out.

In the solitude of the taxi ride home, the finality of it all crushed my chest. It was as though I had lost a dear family member. I walked in through the front door, deadened to my back pain and crawled into my wife's arms.

I huddled under the blankets till after midday the next day. Apparently the world was now my oyster, but I wanted to keep the shell closed. And now, all of my brave yahoo about 'Let's just do it' was firmly on the table.

I edged forward slowly, scanning the net for suitable travelling craft, with no idea what I was looking for or in what country. I'd never even seen inside a motor home let alone bought one. My vision of an air-conditioned luxury coach with a separate parents' bedroom was very quickly modified to the equivalent of a tent with metal sides and wheels. I looked at big motor homes, little ones, old ones and shitheaps that, while affordable, I refused to consider. There was even one with red racing stripes on its sides. The pictures of it looked spectacular.

I soon learnt that our purchase had to be held by a third party because we couldn't own a motor home without an EU passport. This led me to a small business in Holland that would sell us a van and hold the ownership papers. We'd be exposed. They could rip us off at any time. But I was now snorting the travel cocaine, experiencing psychedelic flashes of me driving this wondrous vehicle across foreign lands, and so assured myself the risk was worth it.

It wasn't long until I was made to feel a lot less certain about the trip.

Jaimie's kindergarten teacher declared that a long absence would damage our children's intellectual development. Mandy had just had her first book published, *Family Village Tribe* (the story of Flight Centre and how the company's structure was based on Stone Age tribes), and had been busy promoting it. A 2UE radio announcer asked her if it was responsible taking kids overseas given the recent rise in terrorist acts around the globe. (Unfortunately the higher statistical chances of getting killed in a car outside our front door held no weight in the shock-jock world.)

Horror-stricken parents we knew also pronounced: 'You and your kids? In a van? For a year? I can't think of anything worse! See you in three months... if you make it that long!'

And then there was the Australian government's useful travel warning site. It advised travellers to avoid known terrorist attack targets including houses, hostels, hotels, shopping centres, special events, tourist sites, bars, clubs, cafés, restaurants, airports, schools, churches, banks, car parks and planes. Somehow they had missed motor homes, so we were in the clear – if we could swim there and stay in caves.

All of these opinions just added to my own whispering doubts. *You've committed career hara-kiri. Your kids need stability. You're avoiding the stench of redundancy. Who are you without your respected job title? Money, money, money!*

I started to feel like we were missiles shooting through the skies with a very clear target, and yet a barrage of deflectors were trying to send us off track by attacking our insecurities.

The cumulative pounding of these negativity bombs finally shook my resolve. We hadn't yet bought the van. We could still pull out. 'What have we done?' I asked Mandy one night, suggesting that two kids under five, long-term travel, foreign places and camping in a box together were possibly a stupid cocktail.

'Follow me,' she said. 'Ignore the dream stealers.' She took me by the hand and led me upstairs. I thought it was an odd moment for sex but who was I to question?

On the wall of the bathroom was pinned a giant poster of a walled city fortress hanging over spectacular blue waters. 'I went out and bought this picture today. It's Dubrovnik,' she pointed. 'Croatia.'

I stared at the poster for some seconds, realising that this and other awesome places were suddenly within reach. 'We've gotta go there!' I gasped.

In a final test, a week later the MD offered me another job back at the company.

For a moment I was buzzed about being offered a lifeline back to the corporate ship, but then I realised it was more a net back onto the trawler and I was the prawn. As that realisation dawned, my smile broadened. For Mandy and I, in wine-soaked revelry, had pressed the button on our computer the night before. With a gasp of exultation, we had wired 14,000 euros to Europe to buy a motor home.

It was too late. 'Appreciate that,' I replied to him, knowing I was about to cut the line forever, 'but no thanks. The company isn't the vehicle for my future anymore.' Mandy and I had another vehicle in mind for that.

It was now my chance to live out my dream. From now on when I spoke of 'we', it would be about me and my family, not the corporate 'we'.

My back going snap and my job going poof had produced the unwanted perfect storm that landed me in the doorway of an old windmill on a farm somewhere in Holland. And for a brief moment, as I flashed back through the previous months, the shock of seeing the motor home receded. I was still smiling, sensing I'd been given a gift. Except I had no idea what I was supposed to do with it.

I didn't know what this trip would produce. Maybe it would be a lengthy indulgence. Maybe it would be like a visit to a carnival ride, and afterwards I'd return to my seat in the main circus with nothing changed but a better photo album.

What I did know was that I had dreamt of this trip since I was twenty-two and now I was going to do it. Albeit in a slightly bigger and more dilapidated van, with a wife, two children and with less time than I had originally planned in the Hofbräuhaus. But I was frothing with excitement. We were no longer going to live between the lines. We were going to go on the road… with kids!

2

UNRAVELLING

The old windmill on the farm outside Utrecht had, at some time in decades past, been painted purple with red doors. Most of that had now flaked away, leaving spots on its ghost grey timber like faded paint bombs. I entered the shed and walked through the sea of beautiful antique autos towards the brooding ugly sister in the corner. But I didn't want to get close, instead pacing around the giant motor home in slow motion, keeping a cautious distance.

The internet images that drew me in had clearly been like an ageing supermodel's airbrushed photo shoot. The red racing stripes were barely distinguishable through the film of dust. The battery cables to the open engine had certainly not featured before. If this were to be the vehicle that was to deliver us to the promised land, I figured it was going to take more than forty days and nights just to clean it.

I continued staring at the beast as Donna passed me the keys.

'I've partly cleaned her to show you how it might look. See the bonnet.' She pointed with pride.

I leant forward to identify one square section of the vehicle that was gleaming white.

'Come on, let's look inside,' she insisted.

I opened the side door and crossed the threshold as a musty, unrecognisable smell slammed up into my nostrils.

'Whoa!' I scrambled backwards out the door.

'Chemical toilet.' Donna laughed. 'Sometimes they smell a bit when left stagnant for months.'

'Uh huh,' I intoned, not really wanting to know what a chemical toilet was.

But I had no option. For better or worse, we owned this thing. I braved the growing wave of regret and nausea, clambered back in and started exploring. The double bed enclosure above the driver's cabin seemed claustrophobically small, although its tiny mattress was wrapped in plastic, giving me the first spark of hope that something had been maintained.

'Uh huh.' I climbed in hunched trepidation through to the driver's cabin. The basics were there: two seats, a gearstick and a radio. The 110,000 kilometres on the speedo were accurate. I sat in the driver's seat, closed my eyes and put my hands up on the steering wheel. And that was when I felt it. With the wheel gripped in my hands, the road trip became real. I squeezed the wheel tighter. I would steer this machine to another world.

Once the windows were open and the smell began dissipating I grew more interested. I'd never seen inside a motor home before so I tried to pretend I knew what I was inspecting. The inside timber panelling was clean. The kitchen chairs were striking in their faded brown spermatozoa pattern. I bounced my bottom up and down on them and gave Donna an expert thumbs up. The bunk beds at the rear seemed perfect for the

31

kids. There was a cupboard, a little fridge, a sink and two cook tops. But even so, I couldn't stop wondering how the hell the four of us were going to survive in this box together.

The first minimum requirement at least was there: the vehicle existed and our money had not disappeared in a scam.

'So do you like Franki?' Donna asked.

'Who's Franki?'

She pointed at the van. 'It's a Fiat Frankia. 1991.'

'Oh... Yeah... Looks... um, great,' I lied.

I then delved into the second minimum requirement. 'Does she go?'

An hour later I was steering the machine along the motorway back to Utrecht. I had just left a petrol station after almost sideswiping the pumps and smashing into the overhead awning.

'Watch out for the top box!' Donna had called, pointing to the roof.

'What's a top box?' I called back, but she was gone.

I'd never driven a vehicle this size. I was on the wrong side of the road for me and there was no rear window or view. I couldn't judge the distance to the sides, so stuck close to the lines on the left. And even with the added power of the faded red racing stripes, the van struggled to keep up with Donna as she zipped her Fiat through the traffic. I was forced through many gear changes and, as a consequence, my back started aching.

But there was one saving grace. I was behind the wheel, turning it like it was a giant pizza, trucking along in a foreign land with no idea where I'd be tomorrow. Now that the van was a proven goer and the initial shock of the size and smell had worn off, I was slowly warming to the beast.

'Franki... stupid name!' I said out loud to myself. 'I have to come up with a better one!'

I'd always named my travelling vehicles. Roxy had been a baby-shit-coloured Ford Fiesta estate that a friend, Phil, and I had bought in the UK for 300 pounds. We abandoned her outside New Malden station one night with a wad of parking tickets and a few extra dints.

Phil and I also bought Holly in LA for 500 dollars. She was a monstrous 1973 Lincoln Continental two-door pimpmobile we drove and slept in across the States. She oozed along like a boat on an undulating ocean. We abandoned her when the engine caught on fire in the streets of New York.

Hopefully, abandonment wasn't to be the motor home's destiny.

Back at our hotel, I charged into our room thrilled with my first drive to find my family eagerly perched at the window waiting for my report. Then, with a brain to mouth disconnection I was to forever regret, I said: 'Franki will be ready tomorrow!'

'Franki?' they cried back in unison.

I shrugged. 'It's a Fiat Frankia.'

'Oh,' Mandy said in that 'Oh' way that meant that's completely unacceptable and we would discuss it later.

'Franki! We love that name!' yelled Jaimie and Callum. 'Yay!' they cried, jumping up and down on the beds.

We soon rushed out and I pointed to the dirty machine that was our new home.

'Uh huh,' said Mandy.

I left her to go on her own voyage of acceptance.

That evening we packed the kids into the double stroller and bounced along Utrecht's cobbled laneways between stone buildings, canals and what seemed a million pushbikes. Jaimie had Scary Dolly, one of the few extravagances we'd allowed her to bring, tucked under her arm. Callum was rugged up like the Michelin man with his little face peering out from under a hood. For them this was a great lark, riding planes and staying in hotels, and they were goggle-eyed, determined not to miss a thing. For the first three minutes anyway, until they fell into a comatose sleep with mouths wide open and drool dribbling down their cheeks.

For Mandy and me, though, it was no lark. Our regular lives had been replaced by a rolling shoebox on wheels that was a borderline shit heap and smelt like it. We parked the stroller in a pub's courtyard, ordered two huge blonde beers and clinked glasses, ignoring the doubts we could see in each other's eyes. I also ignored my back pain, deciding not to tell Mandy that the pumping of Franki's clutch had reignited it. If I did, she would rightly insist I not drive, and that to me was not acceptable. I had dreamt of steering a rig like this for years. To be the one behind the wheel on the open road, in charge, singing to the radio, it was all a key part of my journey ahead.

The next morning, knowing the van was waiting, I was desperate to get out of the hotel and on the road. First, Donna insisted she give us the critical 'motor homes for dummies' tour. I relented, accepting that we did need a quick summary of the basics. 'The fridge is a three-way,' she started.

'Is it sexually confused?' I asked.

Mandy slapped my arm. 'Shush!' To Donna, 'So how does it work when we're not plugged into a power point?'

I nodded, supporting what sounded like an excellent question.

Donna pulled out the vehicle's manual, scanned it, and then handed it to Mandy. 'Can anyone read German?'

We shook our heads.

'Oh well,' Donna said, 'don't worry. It's the same as any other motor home you've used.'

'Used?' I barked. 'We've never even seen one before.'

Everything else from then may as well have been explained in Swahili. Water pumps, gas connections, battery lights, back-up battery, wind-out awning, a kitchen table that somehow turned into a bed, dual water tanks, a plethora of keys, two types of power cords, a bike rack, and the top box, ingeniously named I thought, as it's a box, on the top. And finally Donna came to the chemical toilet and how to clean it.

'Woo woo, stop there,' I interjected, still traumatised by the overpowering smell from the day before. 'What do you mean, clean the toilet? Doesn't it just sort of flow out as we go or something, like when you're pissing on an old train and you can see the track flashing below?'

Their faces turned to me as though I needed special care. 'It's a cartridge.' Donna spoke very slowly for my benefit. 'When it's full, you empty and wash it.'

I shuddered, disgusted at the concept of this designer poo bucket.

As the baffling instructions continued, the kids set up camp inside the bunk beds, ecstatic in their cubby-like abodes. Mandy paid diligent attention and kept asking pertinent questions which resulted in a lot of useless reviewing of the German manual. She was getting frustrated as she wanted to ensure we knew how everything worked. I was getting frustrated because I hated reading manuals and instructions. That's why I never buy anything from IKEA.

'This looks important.' Mandy pointed at a red flashing light.

'Car alarm,' Donna said.

'How does it work?' Mandy asked.

More manual reviewing, more non answers. The van reconnoitre burst through the hour barrier and by then I was completely disinterested in the instructions, and just itching to get on the road.

'It can't be that hard,' I announced. 'Let's just go and work it out.'

'We've only got one chance to find out,' Mandy insisted.

Our eyes met in that way that happens when you both want to have a fiery debate but you can't because you are in public.

'No worries, she'll be right,' I said.

We eventually negotiated a compromise. We would go to the nearby Utrecht campsite and spend three days there learning how the machine worked. The umbilical cord back to Donna would be maintained if we needed help. Secretly I was relieved that my scant knowledge of motor homes was not to be tested.

I tossed Mandy the keys and she grabbed them with joy, unaware my gallant offer was due to pins and needles zinging in my foot. We climbed into our new home, strapped the kids in, cranked it up and pulled out. I started singing Willie Nelson's 'On the Road Again'.

Our dream was now a reality but within minutes we entered a firestorm of traffic on Utrecht's ring road and rain started slapping down in chunks. This was Mandy's first turn behind the wheel and she too was struggling with its size and being on the wrong side of the road. 'I can't see! How do the wipers go? And the side mirrors are pointed all the wrong way!' she yelled.

I leant across her, blasted the horn by accident, and bumbled around with various knobs, turning the radio, air vent and lights on and off till I found the wiper control. 'Got it! No worries. See. Everything works!'

The wiper blades, bald of any skerrick of rubber, then arched slowly across the windscreen, screeching like fingernails on a chalkboard, our heads following them.

Twenty minutes later, I should have been singing 'Off the Road Again', as we scampered into the Utrecht campground like frightened rabbits into a hole. The dream road trip would have to wait a bit longer.

We were directed to a soggy rectangle of space and it was now time to put our newly learnt camper skills into action. Mandy had a tool box at home. I once broke three light bulbs trying to change one. It was fairly obvious who the practical expert on this trip would be, and so I isolated what I thought would be the easiest chore, winding out the awning. I jumped out the door, splatting into the mud, to find the awning fixed in place. Rattling and pulling at it till it almost snapped I eventually called for help. 'Watch out as you jump out, though. It's quite a drop. You'd think the silly bastards would have put a step in or something.'

Mandy looked at me, shook her head, bent down and pulled out a step that was levered under the door entry.

'Oh what a good idea! I must have missed that in Donna's induction.'

She then wordlessly walked past me and unclipped the fastener that held the awning in place. 'Huh. Good design. I was gonna do that next,' I said.

The kids were huddled in Callum's lower bunk and playing with their drawing boards. This suited us as it kept them out of the way. I plugged in the power and to my great relief the fridge started and I had actually made a contribution.

With everything set up I went inside and turned on the tap to make some tea. After a moment's delay, an electronic grinding reverberated through the van till bits of dirt coughed out. 'We have no water!' I yelled. 'What else doesn't work in this clunker?'

Mandy interjected. 'Maybe the water tanks are empty?'

I stared at her for a few seconds. 'Oh, tanks. That makes sense.'

We repacked the van, closed all the windows, pulled in the awning, stair and muddy power cable and drove around the campsite to the water station. I directed Mandy to park next to the tap, got out, opened the hatch and then stared stupidly at it. There were two holes.

'I was right,' I yelled, 'Franki's a girl!'

I didn't know which hole was for the water tank and there was also no hose to link the tap to the tank. Again Mandy stepped up. 'They're both for water. One's a reserve tank.'

'Oh. That's a good idea, isn't it?'

She just rolled her eyes and walked away.

My suggestion of filling our hands and chucking water at the holes was never going to fly so I scurried over to a van plastered with Great Britain stickers and asked to borrow a hose.

An hour later, as I was finalising our set-up in the steady rain, I pulled out the stair and made another discovery under the van. 'Hey look! There's a tap outlet here. What a great idea. Handy if we want water outside for cooking!'

'That's the waste tap,' Mandy said.

'What's a waste tap?'

Cold and wet, I headed for a hot shower. On entering the toilet block I was instantly engulfed by wafting smoke. A few guys were scattered around smoking joints. I wandered into a shower recess, stripped off and turned the taps. But nothing happened. I then spotted a box on the wall with a coin slot. 'Argh,' I grunted.

I redressed, went back through the rain, grumbled to Mandy about paying for showers, returned, stripped down again and stuck a coin in. It didn't fit. The slot had a squiggle in it. 'Argh!' I grunted again.

I redressed, trudged back to reception, bought a token for two euros, grumbled about having to buy tokens for showers, bypassed the pot smokers and returned for a timed two-minute drizzle of warm water.

Mandy and I huddled inside the van that night, drinking wine and congratulating ourselves on getting this far. The kids were tucked into their bunks and fell asleep fast. All was finally calm, our first night in our new home. But it was cold and getting colder. I insisted on turning on the gas heating.

'Do you know what you're doing?' Mandy asked as I started twisting and tweaking various knobs.

'Yeah, yeah. Easy-peasy.'

The gas machine was at floor level and faced into the little hallway opposite the children's beds. I clicked and clicked away and eventually it sparked into life.

'Got it,' I called triumphantly, relieved at finally getting something right for the day. The machine then started building into a loud whirring sound like a helicopter preparing for take-off. Then, after a series of spluttering coughs, dust spurted out from its vents all through the van. We jumped up, screaming, and ran around opening the windows to the cold night air. Rain swept in as the dust storm dissipated. The kids slept.

I felt like this whole experience was slowly unravelling on us.

Finally we climbed up into our bed above the driver's cabin and huddled together to keep warm.

'Let's just go to sleep,' I said. 'It'll be easier tomorrow.'

But the bed recess seemed matchbox small. I had never been a cuddler. I liked my personal space and now found that with every movement I would crush into Mandy or thump my head against the low roof. Each time she moved I thought I was going to be pushed out onto the kitchen table below.

'You'd think the silly buggers would have something to stop people falling out,' I complained.

Mandy leant across me and pulled up a wire net and clipped it to the ceiling.

'Oh what a good idea,' I said.

I pulled the curtain closed across our vestibule, realising this thin red cloth was to be our bedroom door providing peace, privacy and sleep for the next year. Yet sleep didn't come.

After some insomniac hours of claustrophobic madness, I had just drifted off when Jaimie was woken by sporadic bursts of laughter from nearby tents filled with pot-smoking European students.

'I need to go to the toiley!' she cried.

'OK,' I called back.

'But I can't get down!' She was in the top bunk and unable to undo the netting. 'And I'm scared to go in there.'

I clambered down, wondering whose stupid idea this van was, unclipped her net, and stood half asleep in the cubicle while she finished her business. I tried to flush the toilet but it was jammed, so I just gave up and left a puddle of wee in it.

Back in bed I fell deep asleep, but was snapped out of this trance when Callum cried out later. It was Mandy's turn. She rolled over me under the low ceiling like we were playing a game of Twister and kneed me in the head on the way through. We never fell back to sleep.

The next morning our bleary eyes and weary bodies were evidence of the torture of sleep deprivation. The kids climbed up into our bed and we all huddled in the cool morning air, hiding under the blankets from this new reality.

In the end I climbed down and started boiling water for coffee. Turning to set up the cups, I bashed my knee on the kitchen table. 'Faaark!' I hissed out quietly so the kids wouldn't hear me swear.

I dropped to the floor, not noticing that Mandy had climbed down and opened up the high cupboards. I stood up and promptly knocked her backwards into the driver's cabin, her arm whacking the not yet boiled water off the burners. I launched up, thinking it was scalding water, and slammed my head into the corner of the cupboard she had opened. 'Shit! Shit!' I yelled not so quietly this time as blood ran down my face.

'What's the matter, Daddy?' The kids' faces innocently peered through our curtain from above.

This question had so many answers on so many different levels. I stared at them for a long moment. 'Nothing. Nothing at all.'

The dream stealers were right. This was bloody terrible. We couldn't take this for long.

We desperately needed a diversion from the hellish reality of camper living and it was not far away. Mandy's best friend, Chrissie, and her yet-to-be-viewed new boyfriend, Martin, were arriving from the UK.

Mandy had met Chrissie in London in the early nineties when they'd both lived in a shared house. They'd generally avoided each other till one day Mandy crept into Chris's room to borrow something. Inside she discovered a beautiful writing desk and a treasure trove of books scattered over the floor. Mandy, who started reading under her sheets by torchlight at age four, and Chris, who was a playwright, instantly recognised they were kindred spirits.

Chrissie had spent her working years denying herself money to follow her dream of writing, so we needed her to remind us to follow our quest, as hard as it gets. When she arrived at the Utrecht railway station, we waited a respectable moment and then flung ourselves at her.

She and Martin distracted us from the ongoing torture of broken nights and cramped living conditions and, with security in numbers, we decided to cut the umbilical cord and drive north to Amsterdam.

Mandy insisted that since it was peak season we had to call and book in advance but her mania for planning offended me. It was one of our Mars/Venus things. 'That's bullshit,' I snapped. 'I'm not doing that. That's like planning and rules and regulations. Lines, man, lines! I'm here to wing it and escape that crap. We'll just turn up. We'll be right. No worries.'

She interpreted the craziness in my eyes and relented.

When we arrived at Gaasper Camping, a line of campers blocked the gates. Before the obvious was said, a chap on a pushbike cycled up and started blabbering on in Dutch.

'English,' I replied. 'We *sprechens* English.'

He pointed at our vehicle plates. 'Not Nederlander?'

'No, no. Oz-tray-lee-ann.'

'Oh, I'm sorry. We are full. You should have booked in advance.'

I tried to ignore Mandy's laser-like death stare, as a thought hit me. 'Put the kids on your laps where they can be seen,' I whispered to Chrissie.

I turned back to the man. 'Our kids in the back are really tired,' I said in a most desperate tone. 'Is there nowhere you can squeeze us in?'

He leant inside to see our two little children propped up as cute as infant models in an Anne Geddes' calendar. 'One minute, please. I will see.'

Ten minutes later I was winding out the awning all by myself, smug with my non-planning success and suddenly thinking the kids could come in very handy. I connected the power, pulled down the well-designed step, and clicked the fridge on. I was starting to get the hang of all this until I opened the refrigerator door and a gush of water flowed out. I had assured everyone I'd changed the fridge to gas before we'd driven off but now remembered I had also turned the gas off.

Gaasper Camping was pristine with beautiful grassed campsites. I had never seen such a facility. It had a restaurant, bar, supermarket, laundry and great hot showers. The sun was shining and, for the first time since arriving, we were able to sit outside. Chrissie and Martin set up their tent nearby and Jaimie and Callum ran around squealing, happy to be outdoors.

We had all been to Amsterdam before and had little interest in the tourist attractions, preferring to enjoy each other's company. Still I pushed for one activity, one that would remind me I was not a conventional parent stuck between the lines. And one that promised another short-term diversion from reality.

I made my way down the Avenue Damrak, the human river that was the thoroughfare between Amsterdam's central railway station and the city centre. I navigated past bikes, buses and clanging trams, and eventually bounced down some stairs into the blackened smoke-filled cave that was the Bulldog Café.

Inside, TV screens beamed sports. People were sitting at a long bar drawing deep on rollies like they were sucking thickshakes through straws. Rolling instruments, ashtrays and satchels of dope were laid out before them. The repetitive 'boomp boomp boomp boomp' sound of the 1970s video game Space Invaders thumped out from a darkened corner.

'Hey man,' I drawled to the bartender in an attempt to appear uber cool.

He raised his eyebrows and clearly thought I was a dickhead, before directing me to press a button on the counter which lit up a previously unseen menu of marijuana and hashish products. I reviewed it, trying not to look completely ignorant, and pointed at the cheapest thing I could understand. I handed over eleven euros and the lovely counter lass wrapped the pre-rolled joints in a little gift bag as though I had bought a piece of fine jewellery. Defying the hypnotic pull of Space Invaders, I scurried out having made my score.

That night we put the kids to bed and pulled across the only improvements we had made to the van since buying it: curtains to divide their bunks from the rest of the van.

'Soundproof curtains,' I declared, trying to ease Mandy's parental guilt as she insisted someone had to remain the responsible adult. She had a Bill Clinton toke of the joint being passed around. Yet very soon we were all guffawing uncontrollably after I had congratulated Martin on not having two heads like Chrissie's previous boyfriends; clearly the funniest thing we'd all heard in our entire lives. The kids slept on behind the soundproof curtain and, after we calmed down, we found we'd only shared half of one smoke; we were far from experts. But we'd done something naughty, broken the rules, and for that alone, I felt a little better about what the trip ahead might bring.

Our diversion, however, was soon over. We waved Chrissie and Martin off, holding the kids' hands and staring at the back of their train till it disappeared, realising that we were now on our own. No more umbilical cords.

'What do we do now?' I asked out loud but more to myself.

'Well, we've talked to the kids for months about Santa and the place where the sun never goes down. Why change that?' Mandy replied.

I nodded, saying it over in my head: *the North Pole! Go to the North Pole*. It sounded so ludicrous and far-fetched, so beyond the lines, it was perfect. And so we had a quest – to go to the top of the world.

We spent the rest of the day buying hoses, pillows, an electric heater, a pushbike with two kids' seats, torches, windscreen wiper blades, kids' galoshes, cutlery, warm bedding, toy boxes, food and a crate of one-euro bottles of wine from Aldi.

The next morning we went through our first real departure ritual.

'It's a man's job to do the toilet, you know,' Mandy said.

I pointed out that I couldn't carry it with my dodgy back because it would be too heavy.

'Yeah I know,' she nodded. 'Just wishful thinking.'

'Anyway, don't worry. It can't be that bad, can it?' I said.

We secured the windows and children in place and drove to the water station. I started filling the tanks, pressing my ear to the wall to gauge when they were full.

'Daddy?' Jaimie was hanging out the door.

'Quiet, honey, Daddy's very busy.'

'But Daddy?'

'Shh, this is important.'

Water then exploded all over me and overflowed across the road. I went inside to get a towel and Jaimie pointed at a small light flashing 'full' that she'd been trying to tell me about.

I looked at the digital tank level display installed to avoid the overflow flooding I had caused. 'Oh… well, that's a good idea, isn't it?' I scampered outside, declaring Jaimie officially Tank Girl, which produced a beaming smile of pride.

I then leant under the van to check out the waste outlet that I now knew stored run-off from the sinks and shower. 'We have to get this exactly over the drain,' I called out knowledgeably and proceeded to direct Mandy to park right above it. I turned the valve and a stream arched powerfully out over the grid, shooting murky water and small chunks of food bits with their own unique smell onto the bitumen, washing across the street with the water overflowing from the tanks. Other campers watched on in horror.

Meanwhile, Mandy had extracted the chemical toilet canister. It was full and smelly and, as she heaved it up, small bits of fluid spilled out of a tiny air hole onto her.

'Oh my god!' she screamed, dropping the box and running in a circle as though she was being attacked by a swarm of killer bees. 'I'm spilling shit all over myself!'

I looked the other way, stifling a grin and holding the hose.

Eventually she got into a lifter's squat position and heaved the heavy box up, holding it as far out in front of her as possible, as though she were carrying a ticking bomb. It sloshed around as she stumbled along with its weight straining her arms. 'I hope you're enjoying this,' she gasped as she went past. 'Because if you keep grinning like that… I'm going to stick that hose up your bum.'

She stopped three times to put the box down before getting to the waste room, a dedicated place for the camper vans' faeces and piss. I had peeked in there the day before and been blasted with the smell of raw sewerage. Mandy gagged, held her breath and entered, heaving the box upright to pour out its contents. Then she repeatedly washed it, completely emptying all the water out and resealing it. That activity wasn't in any travel brochure.

She came out pale and sweating. 'That is the... singular... most disgusting thing I have ever done in my life!' she panted. 'You better get your back right, hose boy, because I'm not doing that for the rest of the trip!'

For the first time in months I was somewhat glad I had a stuffed back. 'At least we've sorted how the toilet works. I'm glad that's behind us,' I laughed, patting my bum. 'Get it? Behind us?'

Mandy gave me an unamused glare as she wiped liquid poo from her sleeves.

We eventually packed everything away and drove up the path and out through the campground gates. I had maps everywhere. Water bottles were filled. Tick. The kids had drawing books. Clean toilet. Tick. Tick. We looked like we knew what we were doing. Only Mandy and I weren't deceived. We had no idea what we were doing. And had we known how the next few weeks would evolve, we may not have left the campground.

3

ON THE ROAD WITH KIDS

We stood at the midpoint of the monster Afsluitdijk dyke late that same day. It was sixteen kilometres to either end. The North Sea pounded behind us. The inland sea was calm. I looked back at the road we had come along. It disappeared off in both directions into a blurry horizon. The symbolism was not lost on me. The trek we had taken to get here was now irrelevant. The path ahead led to the unknown.

The dyke was impressive, part of a waterway system regarded as one of the seven engineering wonders of the modern world. Apparently the Dutch had been trying to hold back the waters of the North Sea since medieval times. They built dykes, canals, sluices and windmills to pump water to keep lands dry. From that, they created polders – tracts of land reclaimed from the sea. But some repeatedly and spectacularly flooded, like in 1421 when seventy-two villages were washed away. With almost one third of the country below sea level, you'd think they might have given up, but this dyke was testament to their persistence.

Prior to World War I, the German Emperor was said to have boasted to Wilhelmina, Queen of the Netherlands, that his guards were seven foot tall and hers stood only shoulder high to them.

She had smiled and replied, 'Quite true, your majesty. But when we open our dykes, the water is ten foot deep!'

I leant into the wind and felt the ghost of Wilhelmina's chutzpah rubbing off. Somewhere in that misty distance, I knew I too had to reclaim my own polders – the bits of me that had been underwater for too long. I told myself that just getting on the road would sort everything out. I really wanted to believe that.

I still hadn't told Mandy about the extent of my unrelenting back pain and for the next few days she did all the driving, curious but unquestioning at my apparent lack of interest. I was still clinging to the hope of taking over as master driver soon. But I couldn't even sit in the passenger seat for long and kept disappearing up to our bunk feigning tiredness. For hours I would lie up there, peering out the tiny side window at the green fields and steeple-shaped roofs flashing by. This wasn't how it was supposed to be. As each day passed, I was increasingly bad-tempered and could feel frustration building up inside me, just like the overpowering smell building up in the van.

'There's something really off in here,' I called down.

The wind was gushing in through Mandy's open window below and she couldn't hear me. 'What?' she called out.

I leant over the bed edge and called louder. 'Smell! Poo!'

'Yeah! I've got my shoes!'

My yelling wasn't solving the problem so I climbed down and ventured through the van, hanging on to the walls as we lumbered along. The kids were strapped in at the kitchen bench seats, drawing pages and pages of tiny circles.

'Can you guys smell anything?'

Jaimie pointed to the toilet.

I opened its door and launched back, the smell bursting out as though I had uncapped a sewerage outlet.

'What's that smell?' yelled Mandy from the front.

'The toilet,' I snapped back. 'Did you think to empty it today?'

'Yeah, this morning!'

An overwhelming desire to scream came upon me like a wind squall. This transformation seemed to be happening to me almost daily. 'Well,' I whirled on the kids. 'Did anyone have a poo in it afterwards?'

'Callum did,' Jaimie said.

I stared at him like he'd committed a crime. He started welling with tears, preceding a small sob.

'It's not our fault,' Mandy called. 'That's what they're designed for. And stop blaming us for everything.'

I breathed deeply trying to remain in control, and slammed back into the front seat. 'This van sucks!' I blurted. 'It's all right for you. You get to drive and see things. I have to lie up there in my fucking coffin looking out through a window the size of a postal slot. And those toilet fumes are gonna kill us!'

Surprisingly, I was deemed bad company and soon returned to the prison of the top bed, occupying myself by attempting to interpret the toilet section of the German vehicle manual. When that failed I just stared at the roof. Thinking.

I needed some space. These walls were closing in on me. At home we had our own bedrooms, a separate TV room and babysitters to call on for a few hours' escape. We were constantly entertained by movies, TV, computers, wads of toys and lots of company. We were always busy, always had something to do. Sure, we would go days without spending more than a few hours together, often only being occupants in the same building and never talking to each other in any real sense. But now we were living together without all these distractions, apparently living the dream, able to talk, play and interact for days on end, and yet all I wanted was my home comforts.

Still, I knew I had been a prick, so when we stopped to wander the medieval town of Lübeck in north Germany, I decided to make amends. 'Let's eat out,' I declared.

We went in search of a restaurant serving Wiener schnitzel, but it soon became obvious that our budget, a strict one that had to last a year, would not stretch to many dinner outings. The romantic notion of renewing our backpacker past, when bread, cheese and ham was a treasured staple, suddenly seemed far less appealing than having a steady income and no budget constraints.

'Eight euros,' I suggested.

'For what?' Mandy asked.

I calculated this was the maximum we could pay for a meal each at a restaurant, based on one outing per week with the kids sharing a meal. 'That's twenty-four euros, once per week.'

'It is a holiday, you know,' she replied.

In a miracle discovery we found a place that served Wiener schnitzel for under eight euros. 'See, we can do it. It won't be that hard,' I said.

We spent exactly 24 euros on our food and then sucked down six beers that cost more than the meal. We were unpractised at self-denial.

At the campground that night, Mandy and I strolled over to some fellow campers who were lounging in the most impressive tilt-back camping chairs I had ever seen. I instantly vowed to get one but was more interested in the information these experienced camper types could provide. They immediately greeted us in a blabber of Dutch.

'Nein, nein. No Nederlander. We are Oz-tray-lee-ann.'

'But the "N"?' they pointed at our number plate with an 'N' on it.

After a long introduction I eventually explained our stinky dilemma. 'Is there a trick to these chemical toilets? Ours always smells.'

'Smells? Nooo,' a woman named Gertrude drawled in that odd Germanic English that sounded like playful singing. 'You just empty de kanister and vash eet out.'

'Ya,' Mandy interjected. 'But ve've been doing that.'

'Den you poot some vasser back een eet.'

'Vasser?'

'Oooh ya. And add in de kemeekals to dissolve your vaste.'

Mandy and I, dumb and dumber, looked at each other in a simultaneous ping of recognition. Slowly I advanced the next question. 'What exactly do you mean... put some vasser in? And add kemeekals?' I found myself speaking Germanic English by osmosis. They blinked in confusion as I went on. 'We thought you just emptied eet, dried eet out and used eet.'

They almost fell off their luxurious tilt-back chairs. 'Come,' Gertrude waved, 'I show you.' She took us into her van and gave us a lesson, Chemical Toilet 101, and provided a sample of the chemicals.

'It seems obvious, doesn't it?' I said to Mandy later. 'Shitting and pissing directly into a dry box and then leaving that to fester for a few days is going to smell.'

'Yeah,' she added, as stunned as I was. 'And there really are chemicals for chemical toilets!'

'Who would have thought?' I gasped. 'What another good idea.'

We went shopping immediately and by morning the van smelt as fresh as the green fields around us and we had enough stock of chemicals on board to dissolve a dead horse in a dam.

Freshening the toilet was good, but it didn't relieve my overall edginess. In camp the next afternoon, Jaimie and Callum were on the floor of the van putting together jigsaw puzzles. As he neared completion, Callum realised he had lost a puzzle piece. Now ordinarily this would not have seemed a big issue but he had recently developed an endearing quality when he didn't get what he wanted – an ear-piercing scream. The two-year-old's weapon of choice! He started on a high whistling screech that only dogs, parents and anyone within a half-mile radius could hear. At home this siren passed mostly unnoticed with the benefit of thick doors. In the van it was like he was screaming inside a cave and that cave was my head.

Desperate to stop this wail I crawled around under the table scanning the floor for the piece. But he kept screeching until the noise penetrated into my brain as though repeatedly fired from a nail gun. I flopped on the floor and quivered. 'I am trying to help you... mate.'

I wanted to rip his tongue out. I had to get away. I bashed my head under the table and dashed outside into the field.

'Go and help him,' Mandy innocently waded in at the most inopportune moment.

'I just… did!' I wheeled on her. 'Go and help him your bloody self!'

His scream peeled out again.

'Shhhh–itt! Here we go again! This screaming is driving me fff… mad!' I clenched my fists and stormed back into the van, rocking it as I launched in.

'Johnny, don't!' Mandy cried.

'Stop. The. Screaming. Callum!' I screamed at my son, a technique oddly omitted from the book *How To Raise Boys*.

In reply, Callum screeched back louder.

Jaimie started crying. 'Help him, help him… find the jigsaw!' she sobbed. 'He can't find the last piece, Daddy!'

My eyes bulged as I yelled at both of them. 'Shut up! Shut up! Both of you!'

Jaimie burst out crying.

Mandy interceded. 'What are you doing?'

'Piss off!'

'Piss off you!' she fired back.

Everyone was squealing in some form. I stormed out, waving my arms. 'I'm over this fucking van… And that fucking jigsaw. And all of you! I don't know why we did this trip anyway. It's unnatural, living together like this. I'm outta here!'

I charged off into the nearby woods, pacing around mumbling. I was losing control. I had just said fuck in front of my kids. That was fucked. This camper caper was driving me mad. I desperately wanted a full night's sleep without someone snorting, snuffling or crying. 'It's not much to ask,' I yelled to the trees. I wanted to pee in a toilet that flushed.

I wanted to cook something, anything, in an oven, not a pot. I needed to call someone, but I had no friggin' cell phone. I wanted to check my email, but had no internet. I wanted to get a babysitter and go out, but we knew no one and couldn't afford it anyway because we were on some idiotic eight-euro budget for a schnitzel.

I dropped down in the grass, my head between my knees. And my job was gone. Silence invaded. The seconds tick-tocked. I thought I was over that, but the sting of redundancy, the divorce from the company, still hurt. It had been part of my being for so long, and without it I was lost and nondescript.

And my back was stuffed. More tick-tocking silence.

My back was stuffed. Zinging... pinging... I could do nothing useful. Couldn't carry bags or the kids. Sex, particularly in a camper, had become an abstract concept from a distant past. And I couldn't drive. How was this living the dream? Would I need an operation? Could we even continue to travel? I didn't know and I was scared.

I came back very sheepish an hour later. I don't know why sheep get blamed when I make a dick of myself but that's their burden. I had my own. I had never spoken to my kids or Mandy like that before.

As I entered the van, Callum smiled and held up the jigsaw piece: 'Found it, Daddy. We finished the puzzle.'

I smiled unhappily back, wondering how kids could bounce back so quickly while I was left in a splattered pile of guilt. 'Oh good,' I said. 'Maybe you can work on me next?'

'You're not a puzzle,' Jaimie giggled.

I was to me. I looked across at Mandy. 'Sorry,' was my inadequate statement. 'This whole existence,' I mumbled, 'is like going through a reprogramming. We're on some sort of bizarre family interaction course… except… I'm failing.'

'I understand.' She gave me a hug, letting me off.

Did she understand? If she did she was doing better than me.

We were soon on the road again, an activity I clung to because it instantly distracted me from my thoughts and my frustration at not being able to drive. As we approached the Baltic Sea at Puttgarden in Germany, my mind wandered, developing romantic images of the ferry ahead being a rusty little metal barge with an unshaven sea dog wearing a frayed fisherman's cap and a yellow plastic rain jacket collecting our cash.

'It must be behind that cruise ship,' I pointed as we parked in a long line in the cold misty rain.

The vehicle line started moving forward and Mandy pointed, ecstatic, 'It is that cruise ship!'

The kids leapt into our laps to gape up through the windscreen at the Queen Mary of ferries.

We parked in the hull, climbed the stairwell to the heated passenger deck and explored like kids in a maze, scampering through the restaurants, games room, shops and outdoor viewing decks. We busted the budget again and bought delicacies to eat and glasses of wine. I went into the toilets and stared at the flush cistern as though it had been beamed there from the future. Jaimie and Callum bounced around in a corral of coloured balls while Mandy and I stared mesmerised at a wall-mounted television as though we'd escaped from a lengthy stint in a jungle prison and had never seen one before.

We had only been on the road for ten days but everything about the ship represented lost, decadent luxury. I never wanted to disembark, but when forced to on arrival in Denmark, we decided to continue the treat by selecting the most expensive campsite, splashing out a whole extra five euros per night in the hope it would deliver more fun.

The Charlottenlund campsite was beautifully set in an old fort on the beach just north of Copenhagen. We wedged the van in among impotent but erect cannons and gun turrets that pointed out at the ships plying Copenhagen port. The mid-August weather had turned warm and sunny. After setting up, we grabbed a bottle of wine and wandered across to explore the beach. Jaimie and Callum splashed out ahead in their coloured galoshes that they insisted on wearing even when the ground was dry. I watched them with a smile in my eyes and a little envy. To them this was all fun, simple and uncomplicated. They were hanging out with Mum and Dad, they had their toy boxes and their bunk beds were their own personal fiefdom where a mysterious world of teddies lived. Maybe I could learn from them? Or relearn?

'Watch a kid pick up a rock,' I said to Mandy, pointing at Callum as he did just that, a perfect visual aid to my developing theory on learning from children, before he threw it at a bird. 'Callum, don't throw rocks at birds!' Back to Mandy. 'Anyway, they crouch, bend their knees, keep their back straight and pick up using perfect technique. No one taught them that. They know it inherently. It's only as adults we start bending over to pick stuff up.' The wine was advancing my theory. 'So where did we go wrong? When did we start adopting bad habits when we once knew what to do? When did we stop grasping the zest for life we once naturally had when we were young?' I stated that we needed to be more like the kids, pointing at Callum as he chose that exact moment to shove a handful of sand into his mouth.

Mandy and I laughed and chattered away about eating sand and other important quests like hiding fake dog poo in colleague's desks, moving subtly into a second bottle of wine. It had been a long time since we had babbled on like this, without any reference to schools, nappies, children's medical conditions, screaming remedies, shopping or work. Soon it was 9 p.m., late for the children. I moaned for the umpteenth time that motor homes needed black-out curtains as the northern hemisphere's late summer sun made it impossible for the kids to get to sleep. Mandy left our convivial conversation and went inside to conduct our nightly ritual of hanging towels over the windows to block out the light. She rustled around in there for some time then squealed, 'Johnny, Johnny, come quick!'

She'd never wanted me to do that before! I lurched up and bounced into the van looking around for a snake or a spider.

'Look!' she yelled, and pulled on a plastic knob at the base of a window. Up slid a fitted blind like she was a magician pulling a rabbit out of a hat.

'You're kidding!' I gasped. 'No way!' I ran to another window. 'Oh my god!' I squealed like a teenager, 'There's one here too!' I grabbed another. 'They're on all of them!' I pulled all the blinds up and the van was tossed into midnight darkness. 'What a fantastic idea!'

I instantly imagined long forgotten peaceful nights and even longer morning sleep-ins. Right then, I fell in love with Franki.

In the early 1800s the founder of the Tivoli, the second oldest amusement park in the world built just outside Copenhagen's West Gate, apparently told the Danish king that, 'When people are amusing themselves, they do not think about politics.' So I figured if I was amused, I would not think about my dodgy back, lost career or anything else.

We arrived at the Tivoli gates after making many lavish promises to the kids of the fabulous rides inside. I had not, however, considered the forty euros entry fee.

'But that's about seventy bucks on the Australian dollar!' I hissed to Mandy.

'I don't think we have much choice.' She nodded at the kids.

We had slashed through our budget since touching terra firma with set-up costs, treats and eating out. We simply had to be on a backpacker's budget to stretch the Australian dollar for a year. We had no choice.

'But you promised them,' Mandy said.

I looked at the kids. They were waiting at the entrance, quivering with excitement.

'Yeah, but we have to survive on one hundred dollars a day. That's about sixty-five euros. We can't afford this sort of thing.'

'I know,' Mandy replied. 'But remember the bears?'

The 'bears' was a private code we used to convince ourselves to spend money rather than be sensible and frugal. When we were in Alaska years before, we had chosen to save a few hundred lousy dollars, rather than choppering into the wild to witness a once-in-a-lifetime experience of bears swatting fish at a waterfall. We'd regretted it ever since.

'When are we going in, Daddy?' Callum tugged at my pants.

'It is the Tivoli,' Mandy said. 'We still have to do things and spend some money on the kids. They've been pretty good so far on the big drives and everything.'

I looked at their little eager faces lit up with joy and expectation. It was like staring into the melting eyes of the pussycat in the *Shrek* movies. They could not be denied. I dropped my shoulders in defeat knowing there was only one thing I could do. 'OK, OK. You're right. Hang the expense. We'll start our frugal life tomorrow.' I couldn't let it sit though. 'But we avoid theme parks from now on.'

The kids rode merry-go-rounds and I joined them on boat rides. We watched mini concerts and street theatre. The rides cost extra but by now the money genie was out of the bottle.

We left at twilight to find Copenhagen's centre sizzling with throngs of people soaking up their annual glimpse of warm weather. We revelled in not having to worry about where we were driving to the next day. It was our first real family fun day. We stayed in Copenhagen for five days.

During these days in Copenhagen we found there was nothing to do at night and very soon this had us a little twitchy, desperate for entertainment to fill the void. We needed a fix of something. By the third day the evening dinner became that hit.

It started many hours earlier. We bought fresh ingredients from the local shops. I started chopping vegetables while the kids peeled beans. They grabbed carrot chunks and squealed with laughter as I pretended to cut off their fingers by whacking the knife down hard. Mandy pointed out it was probably not PC to play knife games with kids, but I knew no one would ever find out.

Mandy set the table up outside with cheese and pre-dinner drinks. I fried pork chops, encouraging the kids to give them pet names like 'Choppy' and 'Piggy', before devouring them. We sat outside till it was too cold, listening to music, reading and chatting with other travellers. We then blacked out the home with the fabulous blinds and put the kids to bed.

It was the first shoots of a new evening ritual that developed with the long extended sunsets. Mandy and I would sit on the beach, leaning against each other, looking out across the ocean at the moving lights of the ships, as the kids played around us. One evening, a lovely old couple strolled past romantically holding hands. They wandered out on the short wooden pier, put their arms around each other and pointed at small fish buzzing below the water's surface. It was a peaceful, dreamy moment.

The old chap, who was quite large, then stripped off all his clothes and jumped, spreading his legs out wide, his private parts hanging down like an old ram. His partner dropped her gear and dived into the freezing water as well, giving me a rear view I will never be able to laser off my mind.

'They only go nude because people don't look at them,' I said in my shock. 'If they were cute, people would stare and they'd put their clothes back on. It's a circular farce.'

This prompted us to chat for hours about Scandinavians' propensity for public nudity and many other critical world issues. And as each night went, our chats became increasingly long but on a surface level, like the first few dates in a courting. Extracted from our busy home life, it was like we were on a 'getting to know you again' course. After a number of these nights, the conversation cracked open.

'I'm not really getting into this trip,' Mandy fired the opening salvo.

I almost exploded with relief to find it wasn't just me carrying doubts. In the frenzied whirlwind leading up to departure Mandy had juggled the kids, packed the house and looked after a pensionable husband while trying to exult in and promote the achievement of her first book being published. 'I still have one more interview to go.' She described how it had been hanging over her like a storm cloud. 'I feel I've had to stay in business mode.'

We were 15,000 kilometres from home but the real world kept dragging Mandy back. For me, I had never left it. My job loss and back were constantly pulling me down.

She talked about how she was also worried about me and my back, what it meant for all of us. Worried about why I was so quick to anger all the time. 'It's not like you,' she said. 'What am I doing wrong?'

Wrong? I couldn't believe Mandy thought she was doing something wrong (apart from her penchant to plan, of course). I was the only nutcase in this tour group and I told her that. It was a long night but by the end we finally felt somewhat united. We'd both spent the last few weeks riding a horse with the reins pulled tight. This communication thing, forced upon us in our isolation, was proving quite a boon.

The next day Mandy sat among the guns and completed her final interview with an Australian radio station. The interviewer loved the book and had even read it, which was rare. Mandy came back and screamed, 'I'm free!' I was happy for her. She'd been paroled. But I didn't feel freed.

The next morning I decided it was my turn to confide. 'I can't drive,' I confessed. 'I can't use the clutch.'

Speaking the words out loud made me feel old and broken before my time.

She knew this was a thundering slap in my face. Tears welled in her eyes.

'It's not so much the not driving that's pissing me off,' I continued, 'I'm not really sure what is. It's sort of everything and nothing.'

'Go on,' she nudged like a good fish-gutting therapist.

'You remember last year when I started golf lessons?' I reminded her how I had once won the club's C grade final, playing a round from the gods, two over after fourteen holes. Golf speak was a foreign tongue to her but she politely pretended to understand the gravitas of this score. 'And for some reason, I never followed through. I went back to social hits, playing like crap. And I lived with that regret ever since.'

'And then?' she prodded again, knowing that getting me to talk about emotions was like getting a cat to bark.

'And then... last year I started lessons and practice. I decided I wasn't going to die wondering. Nothing worse. And then my discs burst.'

She was still, urging me on with her eyes. 'The physio said I still had a golfing future. I could learn an abbreviated swing like an elderly lady golfer. Ha!' I laughed. 'He may as well have sliced off my scrotum with a rusty saw and smashed it with a meat mallet! And now, this… this… coming on the road caper…' A long silent pause. 'I can't drive. That's all I wanted to do. Be behind the wheel of the camper in foreign places. It's another regret, right in my face. Daily.'

Right now, every tiny obstacle felt like a drop that overflowed a full bucket. And I couldn't stop the wave of anger that erupted. 'I know I'm being a turd and taking it out on everyone.'

'Uh huh… the jigsaw,' she said.

'Yeah.'

'And the toilet.'

'Yeah.'

'And –'

'OK, OK. We don't need an audit.'

We sat in silence for some time as I recognised that the jigsaw piece had exposed me. For that outburst I couldn't blame anyone or any imaginary overflowing bucket. I felt I was a failure as a father. I may have been a good provider, but that did not make me a good parent. I had been away at work or mentally absent too often. I had never developed real patience with the kids. Their mum was good at sympathy and understanding, but now I was trapped in this bloody van.

Mandy finally interrupted the silence. 'I'd have the bad back for you if I could,' she whispered.

I remembered again why I had followed her across the world to marry her. 'Anyway, enough of the deep and meaningfuls.' I straightened up like a true blokey bloke. 'Let's get on the road in the morning. We're in Europe. We're lucky. I'll be right,' I lied.

And she accepted the lie. For now.

But the truth was that if we were going to make the distance –
the full year in the van, or beyond, as a couple and a family
– one thing was certain: this trip was going to be my greatest
personal challenge.

4

THE LIGHT AT THE END
OF THE TUNNEL

'Legoland costs seventy euros!' I gasped, clicking off the phone.

Mandy seemed unimpressed so I clarified. 'That's each!'

'Each?'

'Callum's free because he's two. So 210 euros, which is 400 dollars.' I had adopted a habit of converting everything to Australian dollars, and adding a bit when it was convenient to my argument.

We started whispering in hushed tones. We couldn't afford this amount even if it was for something exciting for the kids. Our total daily budget for food, accommodation, fuel and fun was sixty-five euros. I'd insisted at the Tivoli there would be no more extravagance; a Legoland cash explosion was simply not possible.

'But you've been waffling on about Lego for hours.' Mandy nodded towards the kids.

As a result of my encouragement, the children had been chatting animatedly all morning as we drove over the Great

Belt Bridge to the Jutland peninsula. They'd been calling at intervals, 'How long till we get there?' They hadn't been this excited since they'd discovered animal-shaped pasta.

My commitment to exercising a newfound empathy towards the children was under its first major test and I had suckered myself into the ultimate parent trap – the ill-thought-out promise.

I turned to Mandy for guidance but she just shrugged in exasperated defeat. 'What can you do?'

'I dunno.' I looked back into the kids' eyes to see them shining with excitement. Denying the little tykes would be like drowning a puppy. I dropped my shoulders in defeat and breathed deeply, knowing there was only one thing I could do.

'Legoland is closed.'

The resultant howls accurately expressed the kids' opinion but my counterpromise of double-scoop ice creams, any flavour they wanted, soon bought back their favour. Throughout this discourse, Mandy had stared straight ahead, wanting no part of my deception. 'How do you know there's an ice cream shop where we're going?' she whispered.

I looked across at her making a mental note: no more ill-thought-out promises.

The Ribe campsite fortunately had ice cream, and so armed, we visited the site of the 1641 burning of witch Maren Spliid. She was apparently an independent and outspoken woman, unpopular traits in women at the time, who King Christian IV ordered burnt after her torture-induced confession. It wasn't all bad for her though. In a humanitarian act, a bag of gunpowder was strapped to her so when she was tossed into the flames, she would blow up and her death would be quicker.

On the drive north the next day to cross the Norwegian Sea to Kristiansand in Norway, Mandy was vociferous about ringing and booking ahead to check the ferry's timetable and price. I was beginning to wonder if the outspoken Maren Spliid had been reincarnated. 'The bloody thing goes every day.' I snapped at this planning mania that was the anathema to my trip. 'Look, this is gonna be a brilliant shortcut.' We had thousands of kilometres ahead to get to the North Pole and I had found a quicker route. 'Straight north. We'll just turn up. She'll be right. No worries.' As my only role was navigation, Mandy acceded and we motored on for seven hours.

At the docks I learnt the ferry was a budget-crunching 300 euros and had just departed. A day lost and another camping fee wasted. It was painfully obvious that my brilliant shortcut was a financial disaster beyond the Lego threat. Mandy simply raised her eyebrows as the air hung stale with the recognition that had I rung, had I planned ahead, we would have saved a shitload of money and a bucket of time. I was starting to think this planning caper had some credibility, but wasn't about to admit that out loud.

The few days of frivolous sunshine in Copenhagen dissipated into a darkening depression with the budget setback compounding the return of ongoing sleepless nights. I could see no light at the end of the tunnel. It seemed unimaginable that we could go on like this much longer. My concerns were confirmed two days later when, after arriving in Kristiansand, we made a discovery in Franki's toilet.

One of the more dubious benefits of a camper toilet is that your poo sits there like a steaming cowpat until you pull the lever to drop it into the box below. The moments beforehand provide a great opportunity to inspect the turd at close quarters. That fun activity is what Mandy and I were doing together. 'Look,' she pointed, and in the small pile below us, among someone's previous night's deposit, sparkling like diamonds in the torchlight, was a mass of wriggling white worms. We felt instantly itchy and took action, tossing a coin for which of us would go and get worm treatment.

At home this would be a simple procedure. Slink up to the counter like a teenager buying condoms, whisper the request and get out quick before anyone saw us. Mandy lost the toss.

She entered the brightly lit pharmacy and hung back waiting for a lull in the counter activity. 'Worms,' she said quietly over the counter before discovering no one spoke any English.

'We... have... wooorms.' She spoke very slowly, hoping that by enunciating every syllable, the sales woman would instantly be capable of speaking in foreign tongues. 'Have you... an... eey... tablets?'

The lady shook her head and waved another customer over to help interpret. That failed and soon a gaggle of people were crowded around.

Flabbergasted, Mandy had no choice. She bent over and wriggled her fingers around behind her bottom. This started a game of charades. The circle of people started guessing what wriggling a finger up your bum meant and alternately called out words in Norwegian. They conferred, shook their heads and turned back for more clues until finally an old woman yelled 'Orms!' and clapped her hands together as though she had won bingo. Everyone went 'Aaaahh' and then moved two cautious steps back.

When Mandy returned and insisted we had to wash everything and take monster tablets that looked more suitable for horses, it was yet more proof to me that camper living for families sucked and our adventure was the suckiest.

Still, we had little choice but to keep going and cling to the hope that we'd eventually emerge from this dark place. We left Kristiansand early the next day, chugging off directly north on a road that barely existed on the maps. That poor delineation should have been a warning, but as master navigator I was more excited about the geographical shortcut than the reality of the road. The 'highway' quickly deteriorated to a winding narrow path. This did not bode well. Within hours the driving was hard, requiring Mandy's full concentration, constant gear changes and regular passing stops for oncoming traffic.

By afternoon Mandy was exhausted, having wrestled Franki for 180 kilometres over nine hours. My shortcut north from Denmark was looking more dubious by the day and I was feeling more useless by the hour, aware that I couldn't help Mandy by driving because the gear changes would flare up my back.

We crawled on the following day towards Norway's western fjords, passing through green lush valleys, small villages embedded in turf surrounds like hobbit towns, and narrow gorges wet with crashing waterfalls. But the driving was arduous and slow.

As the van ground away in low gear up the first mountain, hairpin turns and watery slipways made the prospect of us sliding over the edge of the road to the depths below all too real. At the peak, there was a never-ending view of snowy mountain tips to the horizon, which drew us out of the van to breathe in the majesty of it all.

'It's so gorgeous,' Mandy said, 'but this driving could kill me.'

We were soon bracing for the next major incline when I saw the prettiest black hole ever and screamed, 'Tunnel!'

Mandy repeated the cry even louder at the instant realisation we could whizz through the centre of the mountain, rather than crawl over it.

'Get down. Get down!' I cried.

The kids pressed their faces to the table, pretending to protect their heads from being ripped off as Franki roared into the tunnel. Blackness descended upon us as though the blinds had slammed shut.

'Shit! Turn the lights on!' I grabbed the dash.

'Where are they?' Mandy cried back.

'How the hell would I know?' We'd never used them! The long daylights meant we had never driven Franki in the dark. 'You paid attention to Donna.'

Mandy's return glare sent a chill through the cabin as though Dementors had arrived and I realised that ploughing a small bus blindfolded into a dark Nordic tunnel was not the most opportune time to begin a blame game.

I quickly unbuckled and felt around the steering wheel, pulling at knobs and levers, activating the wipers, water jets and fan heater, until finally the lights came on.

'Ooooh!' we all chimed in unison as the dark tunnel lit up before us. Looking ahead, the sides were unlike any other road tunnel I had seen. They were craggy and uneven, like blasted mine shafts, and the rocky walls dripped and glistened with rivulets of water as though the weight of the mountain was cracking through. 'I can't see the end,' Mandy said. 'How far does it go? There's no light at the end of this tunnel!'

She had just enunciated my exact thoughts about this entire journey.

We eventually surged out of the darkness into a bright collage of sparkling silver glaciers, impossibly aqua-blue fjords, craggy white-tipped mountains, rushing waterfalls and orchard-filled valleys. It was like a scene from Narnia, without the lion.

When the next dark hole appeared in the mountain side ahead everyone pointed and screamed, 'Tuuuuuuu-nnell!' and in we charged with our heads down and the lights on. From that moment on we became a family of ardent tunnel spotters, swinging between mountains and valleys, virtually the only vehicle on the Norwegian roads, riding the world's greatest rollercoaster.

For a couple of exhilarating driving days, our problems receded as we were immersed in the majesty of the scenery. We rode on multiple free 'cruises' as ferries across the fjords formed part of the Norwegian highway system. We started commenting on each mountain tunnel's width, height, noisiness, wetness, wall smoothness, lighting, degrees of ascent or descent, bumpiness and, most of all, its length. Two kilometres, six kilometres, thirteen kilometres, with a myriad of little ones in between. Mandy and I agreed that size really does matter in tunnel world.

When we finally arrived at the holy grail of tunnels, the Lærdal, its twenty-five kilometres making it the longest tunnel in the world, I was desperate to drive. 'Come on!' I said. 'I've been watching you drive for days. This'll be one of the great driving experiences of the world.' It was my moron gene kicking in. 'Just get me to the entrance. I'll skip gears. I'll flick from second to fifth. No worries.'

Mandy was desperate to see joy back on my face, so eventually agreed, with one proviso. 'Just tell me if the sciatica starts and we'll stop.'

Once I was in the coveted driver's seat, gripping the wheel, feeling the power of control, the surge of adrenalin, I had no intention of keeping that promise. This was my moment in the light.

And light there was. Every eight kilometres inside the Lærdal Tunnel a luminous blue cavern shone like a psychedelic shimmering pit stop deep inside the earth, 2,000 metres below the mountain peak above. We stopped at the second cavern so Mandy could have a turn driving and I instantly knew from the pins and needles tingling in my foot that driving had been a mistake.

But I said nothing and we went on. The kids' heads were drooping as the constant bumpity rhythm of the road and the muted lighting took effect. As we sprung out into the daylight beyond the twenty-five-kilometre mark, my eyes adjusted too late at the T-junction. 'Stop sign!' I screamed.

Mandy slammed on the brakes as a truck roared past.

'Bam!' came the sound from behind.

Callum erupted in tears, blood instantly pouring out of his nose. The kids' seat restraints were only waist belts, so with the sudden stop, his sleeping floppy body had lurched forward, smashing his face into the kitchen table.

I launched into the back, pulled him up and went to cuddle him.

'Noooo!' he held up a hand to my face as though he was a film star. 'Mummy! I want Mummy!'

Mandy climbed through and cuddled and kissed him to silence.

I stepped back, stung by his rejection and watched on as she ascertained nothing was broken. I was accustomed to being second fiddle to Mum in these extreme moments, but had hoped that by now, having spent weeks with the kids, our relationship may have improved. It was clear it had not.

We drove off with a new accessory: a pillow taped to the table.

Our destination, the Fjærland campground, was high up in the mountains at the head of the Fjærland fjord and below two arms of the Jostedalsbreen glacier. The campground's one building sat cradled in the middle of a small glacial plain like a pea inside a bowl. It was cold and icy mist was engulfing us from the mountains.

As we entered the campground the kids pressed their noses to the window. This had become their ritual at each new stop, switching their playground radars on. In this case, their radars beeped and they shot out of Franki towards the playground like they'd been fired from a circus cannon.

It was the end of three glorious driving and camping days and we decided to celebrate, but before I had even opened the wine, a piercing scream rang out across the valley.

Instinctively we ran, Mandy two strides ahead of me, being more accustomed with distinguishing the children's real scream from a fake one.

Jaimie was running towards us holding her hand to her face with blood spilling down between her fingers, wailing, 'Callum... thr-threw a rock at meeeeeeeee!'

Mandy scooped her up and rushed into the van, sitting her on the kitchen table. 'Get the first aid kit.'

I jumped left, then right. 'What first aid kit?'

'Under the seat. Where Donna said it was. Here hold her. I'll get it.'

'No! I want my Mar... meee!'

Mandy soon established it was just a flesh wound and, for the second time in as many hours, she applied cuddles and bandages, while I stood by as wanted and useful as tits on a bull.

Our panic was over, but I could hear the dream stealers. We'd taken our kids overseas to outrageous places and put them at risk. Was that responsible? At home we knew where the hospitals were and could react quickly to any emergency. Here that safety net was gone. We had debated this at length in the comfort of our lounge chairs and chosen not to be paralysed by fear, agreeing that no risk led to no life. But a scream in the mountains quickly replenished the seeds of doubt.

I strolled off, collected Callum from under the slide, and completed a self-styled safety inspection of the playground, noting offending rocks, rusted metal and other potential traps in the weathered apparatus. It was declared off limits, an unpopular decision, and I added 'playground inspection' to 'pillow on the table' as must-do's when travelling with small children.

Going to bed that evening, I couldn't lift my leg to get up into our bunk because of the driving. To Mandy's credit, she never said 'I told you so'.

I decided to sleep on the fold-down kitchen table even though Mandy insisted it looked wobbly and frail. I leant on it and declared it as solid as the Hoover Dam.

At 3.02 am, the kitchen table collapsed.

After being abruptly tilted face first into the fridge door, I walked outside into the freezing half-light and stood staring up at the surrounding mountains, feeling as insignificant as an ant. I cupped my hands and blew mist rings. I figured some people may have been bred for this camping lark but I was clearly not one of them. Dodgy showers, budget blowouts, inability to drive, worms, sore back, sleepless nights, no privacy, smashed noses, bleeding heads and now exploding tables. Not to mention the absence of sex because we were effectively sleeping in the same room as our kids. And that was just this week. If we kept going, what hell was ahead for my pampered middle-class quartet?

On other travel romps, I'd been robbed, drugged, tear-gassed, lost, penniless and broken-hearted. I'd even been shot at in Bethlehem. But this family holiday was making those low points seem like a trip to a Bali day spa. I yearned for my comfortable home life. Mandy was right when we entered that first tunnel – there was no light at the end. I was ready to go home.

The next morning Mandy decided to ride the two kilometres into the village with the kids. I would trail on foot. This delayed the returning home conversation I'd decided to have.

Callum was lobbed in the small seat mounted at the front of the bike, and Jaimie in a larger one on the back.

'Shouldn't you strap her feet into the stirrups?' I pointed at Jaimie's dangling feet. 'She might stick them into the spokes.' I flashed back to my brother Paul almost severing a toe doing exactly that.

'No-o!' Mandy replied as though I were daft. 'She won't do that.' And then she imposed the subtle Mother-knows-best tone. 'Don't worry about it, Johnny. It's under control.'

And who was I to argue? She had been the primary carer since the kids were born. I'd been absent at work most of the time, quite happy to relinquish responsibility. In fact it was easier for me. I didn't have to get involved in the tough decisions. So I took one last glance at the dangling feet, accepted her call and waved them off.

We met up in a café perched over the fjord. It had a cosy fire flickering away and an aroma of coffee and fresh-baked scones drifting through the air. Fjærland had been a target destination ever since we'd discovered that the village was one of fifteen book towns around Europe. The book town brochure stated that their mission was to have lots of second-hand books in small, beautiful villages surrounded by great natural beauty.

It sounded like Mandy's nirvana. She could get lost for hours in a bookshop, let alone an entire village of them. We swapped books in the coffee shop and then went to the post office and found its walls also covered with literature. Every business and home in Fjærland operated as a used book outlet, displaying them in nooks, on walls and on outdoor bookshelves, operating on an honour payment system. The place was simply overflowing with hundreds of thousands of books that were stuffed into any spot possible.

We eventually settled on the floor of one shop surrounded by a sea of novels, peacefully reading away, until a crescendo of noise exploded outside. I looked out to see a herd of people stampeding slowly past. Docked behind them was a gleaming white cruise ship – a real one, not just a ferry – that had travelled through the Sognefjord from Bergen on the west coast.

'Tourists!' I reported with disdain as though I wasn't one. Then the door to our hushed inner sanctum flew open and a distinct New York accent squealed, 'Oh my gaaardd! What a quaint little shop!'

We grabbed our purchases and ran from the madding crowd. Mandy wedged the kids and a mountain of books on the bike. She'd reloaded her reading armoury with sci-fi novels, biographies, period dramas and a few Agatha Christies. I had grabbed anything big that could fill weeks of downtime.

I silently noted Jaimie's swinging feet as Mandy heaved off, the overloaded bike wobbling comically around the corner and out of sight. Moments later a piercing scream echoed through the mountains.

I recognised the scream as real and pounded round the bend to find the bike down, books and kids sprawled on the road and Mandy waving frantically.

'She wedged her ankle in the spokes,' she yelled.

Blood was everywhere. 'Has she cut a tendon?' I roared.

Mandy was in tears, wrapping Jaimie's foot in a shirt. 'I dunno! I've gotta get some help.'

We both knew I couldn't carry her. 'Go. Go!' I yelled.

She scooped Jaimie up and sprinted down the road towards the village, banging on the door of nearby cottages.

Callum was sitting silently beside the bike. I picked it up and put him back in his seat and started pedalling as best I could towards the campground.

A car soon sped past us with Mandy and Jaimie in it and by the time I cycled in, Mandy had Franki's engine running.

'What's going on? Where's the doctors?' I asked frantically.

'Back down the mountain in Sogndal. We have to go now!' Mandy yelled.

'Sogndal? Down the mountain? That's fifty fucking k's away!'

We roared off, leaving behind a pile of tables, chairs, the bike and rubbish bags.

Jaimie was shaking in shock. I knelt on the floor next to her bed, holding the rag tightly around her foot. The bleeding wasn't stopping. I glanced up, concerned about Mandy driving down the treacherous mountain while she was near hysterical. 'Calm down, calm down, drive slowly,' I called.

Our progress was excruciating. We had a maddening stop at a busy road toll, were stuck behind a truck in a long tunnel and had fifty winding kilometres of downhill mountain-edge road ahead. At some points I could have gotten out and run faster.

Jaimie had turned ghost-white and her eyes rolled back into her head. This terrified me more than the crying. I lightly slapped her on the face and started talking to her so she wouldn't pass out. I was making a good show of controlling my panic but was inwardly terrified she was bleeding to death while we sluggishly oozed down the mountain.

'Can you go any faster?' I yelled.

'You told me to slow down!' Mandy called back.

'Yeah, that too. I'm just saying maybe you should speed up, but do it slowly!'

Jaimie's eyes focused on me and she squeaked in a quiet little voice. 'Daddy, Daddy, please help me... my foot, it hurts so much.' A single tear trickled down her cheek. Then her eyes rolled back and her body started quivering.

Oh fuck. What could I do? Could we lose her this way? In the mountains in the middle of nowhere. How imbecilic of us to bring little kids here!

Somehow in the panic, Mandy got the directions perfect and, after what seemed an eternity, we burst into Sogndal's emergency room. Jaimie was snatched up and rushed through giant metal doors and suddenly we were just standing there, the result now out of our hands. Mandy turned and fell into my arms, exploding into the tears she had repressed while driving. Callum, a forgotten appendage during all this, wrapped himself around my leg.

Twenty minutes, the longest twenty minutes of my life, ticked away until the doctor emerged. Jaimie wasn't with him. My heart and breathing stopped. He walked towards us. Then the doors swung open and a nurse carried her out. Her eyes were open, her mouth in a smile with a lollipop. I blew out air like a released balloon.

The doctor explained the details but I heard very little after 'She is OK.'

'She is OK. Shock. Maybe broken foot. Tendons not cut. Deep bruising. Need X-rays.'

I wanted to grab this knight in shining linen by the ears and tongue-kiss him deeply. 'OK, X-rays,' I agreed.

He gave directions on how to get to the main hospital on the other side of the fjord and, hours later, after another journey of tunnels and ferries, his diagnosis was confirmed. Nothing broken, all was OK. But it wasn't really.

I felt physically sick. It was the first time in our parental lives we truly had the shit scared out of us that we might lose one of the kids. And it would have been our fault entirely. I started to moot to Mandy that maybe we should pull out of this trip, but stopped myself. It wasn't the right time. She was too shaken to talk about anything practical for the moment.

We stayed at Fjærland another day before driving further north into Norway. Our guidebook gushed about an arm of the Jostedalsbreen glacier that led to the smaller Briksdalsbreen glacier, so we headed there. The accident dominated our thoughts more than the spectacular drive.

It was a good diversion though. The narrow fjord stretched out for miles, its arctic green water reflecting the blue sky and snow in its glistening flat surface. The fjord's sides rose vertically up hundreds of metres on both sides, closing to a triangular end where the glacier drooped down to the water like an old man's white beard.

We were the only living souls there that night, camped on the water's edge opposite the glacier. I was certain we would struggle to ever find a more beautiful campsite. Callum and Mandy picked wild raspberries, delivering them back to a foot-bandaged Jaimie who received the offerings like a queen, enjoying the pampering a near-death experience demands. We counted twenty-seven waterfalls crashing down around us from the melting glacier above before the cold pumping out from the ice herded us back into Franki's warmth.

The kids fell asleep fast so Mandy and I rugged up and went back outside in the never-ending dusk with a bottle of red. We'd spent the past two days lost in our own thoughts about the accident. For me, Jaimie's scream was fossilised in my mind. The rolling eyes, the shaking, her pleading cry for help and my guilty feeling of uselessness, replayed in my mind as a scene from a horror movie. I thought she could have died on that drive down the mountain. That may not have been true, but it was my reality.

Mandy's silence finally broke. 'Thank you,' she whispered.

'For what?'

She turned and looked at me. 'For the foot stirrups... For not saying I told you so.'

We talked into the night, both thrashing ourselves with guilt. 'I've become so used to making decisions about the kids without you,' Mandy said. 'I should have listened. I never owned a bike as a kid.'

I said it was my fault. I'd seen the foot thing happen before. I should have insisted.

A long silence set in, broken only by the systematic pounding of the waterfalls. It occurred to me how ironic it was that I had been snapping at Mandy and the kids for weeks, blaming them for everything that was going wrong, but now, when it really mattered, we clung together, something we hadn't done for a long time.

'It's a wake-up call,' I finally said, remembering my thinking time on the couch. 'Life can be snatched away in a nanosecond, you know! So why does it take a massive tragedy before we stop and wonder if we are doing things right. I mean, it was an accident... shit happens,' I summarised eloquently. 'Maybe next time we'll do better.'

'Yeah well, next time, maybe I don't make all the kiddy decisions.' Mandy was clearly fighting her own internal battle to release some of the parental role she had come to love. 'We make the calls together,' she said.

I nodded. It would be one small step towards reclaiming our togetherness as a couple and a family. But I also couldn't help wonder if I should be careful what I wished for. I might actually have to do something.

Of one thing I was now certain: all the crap I had been filling my head with – worrying about my back, my job, budget blowouts, sleepless nights, whatever – were all just inconvenient blips when compared with one of us dying. I was embarrassed I had been overcome by such a litany of unimportant things; constantly ready to quit, when the glory of life sat waiting for me if I chose to accept that challenge.

I told Mandy how I'd once convinced a colleague of mine to stay strong when all the bullshit at work had been overwhelming him. I had even started singing the Chumbawamba song 'Tubthumping', about getting knocked down and then back up on your feet again, to him.

'I had to leave my desk of course and go into the hallway,' I explained to Mandy. 'I couldn't sit in the office singing songs down the wire like Lady Gaga. The CEO would think I was a bloody idiot.'

'Your point?' Mandy asked.

'Well it's time I started taking my own advice. Life is difficult. Personal tsunamis will hit,' I told Mandy. 'Like this bike accident. It's time I squared up, accepted that and became ready to ride whatever waves come our way, just like we did together the other day, rather than get knocked down by every ripple.'

We drifted back to silence for a while. The stars above the glacier glittered in the strange long twilight. It was an intoxicating moment of calmness. We were sitting in one of the most beautiful locations on the planet. We were on a great unknown adventure with our kids. There might be some risks, there would be more dangers, we'd make some more silly mistakes and there'd be more parental guilt – joint guilt, apparently, now that we were sharing the decisions. But risks and dangers, bike accidents and all sorts of dramas I couldn't control occurred at home too. As long as we were together, what did I really have to worry about?

I felt recharged, as though I had been lost in darkness for months and could now finally see the light at the end of the tunnel.

I was ready for our adventure to begin in earnest.

5

SLOWING DOWN THE SPEEDING FREIGHT TRAIN

The pass was a narrow mountain road that wound 1,100 metres up to the glacial plateau above. It was as steep as a road could be, with a series of sharp, terrifying hairpin turns. It was prone to rock slides, only open for a few months of the year, and banned large vehicles. But it was the name of the pass that inflicted more fear on the family than the challenge. Trollstigen – the troll's pass!

Callum in particular had become wary of anything to do with trolls since confronting Geiranger village's statue of one such hairy oversized beast. Fortunately I was there to comfort him, judiciously avoiding the legend that trolls eat billy goats and little children and telling him that I'd like to be like a troll as they have the magic to turn into other beings.

'Yes!' Mandy added, showing unparalleled spousal support. 'And Daddy's just like one! They are also slow, ugly, dimwitted and easily tricked!'

I may have been outwitted by my wife but I refused to be put off by the pass and its 'troll crossings' warning signs.

Mandy, however, shuddered at the thought of the treacherous drive and suggested we should go back the way we came.

It had been a journey worthy of a second look. Geiranger was locked away from the world at the end of the Geirangerfjorden, clinging to the water's edge at the feet of the mountains surrounding it. We'd arrived via a ferry, another extension of the country's highway system, taking the same path that the leading cruise ships of the world took, but for a pittance of the price. The ferry had churned twenty kilometres through the polar green waters from Hellesylt, snaking past icy waterfalls and between the 400-metre-high sheer cliffs that bound the fjord, gliding as though through a secret watery passage to a hidden land.

As exhilarating as that ride had been, there was one thing stopping me from entertaining Mandy's return idea. I hated backtracking. It's a travel obsession of mine. The very thought of travelling somewhere and then spending minutes, days or weeks returning along the same path is abhorrent. I would do anything to avoid that.

'Straight up,' I pointed. 'It's our only way.'

'What is it with you and no backtracking?' she asked.

Glad she finally asked, I went off into a long diatribe, describing a wild rollick I had in South America twelve years before when backpacking with mates. I'd been so scared shitless then of riding in decrepit buses through the Andes that I absolutely refused to backtrack, and dedicated my travels forever more to finding shortcuts and circular routes.

Mandy sat next to me on the fjord's edge listening attentively to my ramblings, sipping wine and adding questions. By the time I finished my tale, I was confident she now understood my no-backtracking penchant.

'To clarify,' she said. 'To avoid going back, you almost plunged to your death in a bus; Columbian bandits used shot-up bodies to block the road and rob you at gunpoint; you stowed away in the hold of an old cargo plane, clinging to onion sacks while the drunk pilot glugged Scotch from a bottle; you ate monkey and piranha; and became a tourist front for an illegal Amazon river trade baron...' She paused. 'All because *you* didn't want to backtrack!'

I was starting to suspect she had not completely bought into my travel policy. 'Well,' I said quietly, 'I really hate backtracking.'

Once we had hung the back of the van out over the edge of the first hairpin turn the next morning, I too had reservations. I also desperately wanted to drive. I knew I couldn't because changing gears would twinge my back, but I had come to learn that I was only comfortable with terrifying mountain roads if I was behind the wheel. My anxiety progressively increased the higher we went and grew to near panic when ice patches appeared on the road edges. Because of Franki's weight and suspect clutch, we couldn't start on steep slopes, so Mandy had to get a run up around the curves just to keep going. This added to the 'thrill'. On corners, I pressed my face against the window trying to see the road edge, but there was no surface in sight, just a yawning chasm. 'Oh god,' I hissed, gripping the dash as though trying to snap it. 'Can you drive in the middle of the road?'

This had been my third driving critique in as many minutes, my 'helpful' suggestions increasing in direct proportion to our height above ground level.

I rationally knew that driving advice from husband to wife was a crime up there with infidelity, but I was unthinking, gripped with road-terror fever.

Mandy shot a glance at me. 'Will. You. Shut. Up! And stop telling me how to drive! This is hard enough. I am in the middle and if we went any slower we'd slide backwards. Chill out. Breathe! You're making me nervous! You'll make me crash!'

'It's not my fault you can't bloody drive!'

I didn't say it. Instead I sat rigid like a frozen corpse who had died screaming in fright. Catching the brain explosion before it escaped was the smartest thing I had done in recent minutes, but I knew she knew my thoughts and by the time we made it to the top, driver–navigator relations were at an all-time low. I made a mental note to trust her, or at least make a better attempt at pretending to, in the next sticky vehicular situation – it would be good for my marriage.

We drove on for numerous days, cracking hundreds of kilometres each day. We passed through a town called Hell. We watched the landscape slowly merge from forest into open tundra with snow-capped mountains stretching as far as the eye could see. We crossed the sixty-six degree line and stopped at a sign that welcomed us to the Arctic Circle. 'Velkommen til Polarsirkelen.'

This was a landmark, so with the wind chill creating freezing temperatures, I pulled my jacket hood tight, my unshaven stubble protecting my face, and jumped out into the howling cold. I surveyed the vast territory, fantasising about being a rugged explorer at the gateway to the world's last great frontier. The journey ahead would be remote and uninhabited, promising harsh landscapes, isolation and inhospitable weather. It was for real men. I took a deep intoxicating breath, shuddered, and ran squealing into the heated visitors' centre.

As we plodded deeper north, an inspiring piece of writing in our guidebook made detouring to the Lofoten Islands an irresistible draw. We'd never heard of these islands before, so rationalised there could be no better reason to go. After more research, however, it became apparent that to get to the most southern tip, to Å, the easiest spelt town in the world, we would have to cover about 600 kilometres from the turnoff, and then return the same way. That was some serious backtracking. 'There must be another way,' I insisted, covering myself with maps, furiously trying to find an alternative. Hours later I cried out, 'I found the shortcut!' We'd leave the highway, catch a seagoing ferry direct to Å and then drive north the length of the islands across a series of bridges to reconnect with the mainland.

The response was a stifled groan, my action cry of 'shortcut' apparently now being translated into 'Johnny creating imminent disaster'.

I ignored these vibes, my plan in full motion when we arrived at the docks at Bodø for a ferry to the Lofoten Islands. But Mandy was more concerned about a storm warning we'd heard on the radio.

'No worries. She'll be right,' I said, noting from her look that she seemed to have also lost faith in my calming words of assurance. 'Look at the size of that thing.' I pointed to the huge vessel. 'It would slice through icebergs. And anyway, they'd cancel it if it was too rough,' I said, as though I had intimate knowledge of Norwegian ferry policies.

The main thing for me, though, was that a small storm wasn't going to cause us to miss the only boat in three days that would save us over 1,000 kilometres and many days of backtracking. I'd do anything to avoid that.

There were no other tourists in line. Brawny unshaven men wearing rubber boots and woolly clothes huddled around salt-rusted trucks and tray backs. The vehicles and the cod fishermen both looked weathered by the sub-zero fishing lifestyle.

We drove on last and the big steel doors closed behind us, then we climbed the stairs to the passenger deck. At the top, I turned and noticed the staff were running steel cables through all the vehicles' wheels and bolting them down to the floor.

'They didn't do that on the other ferries.' I frowned.

A burly bearded chap saw my inquisitive look. 'Storm coming,' he growled. 'Could be a bit rough.'

There was something about the way he said 'a bit rough' that reminded me of Australian outback farmers and their cool tendency towards understatement when faced with major problems. I decided not to share this thought with Mandy.

Within minutes of the boat entering the unprotected waters of the Vestfjorden for the ninety-kilometre crossing, my suspicions were confirmed. The big craft started bobbing like a toy in a bathtub, attempting to surge on into the open waters. As the ferry scooped down between the giant waves, we could only stare into a wall of water in front. The boat would then launch up at an acute angle and crash through the crest, only to ride down the back of it and start a slow swoop into the upward curve of the next wave.

People were stumbling and falling across the deck. Mandy soon turned as white as the foaming sea froth, her hand covering her mouth. 'You... watch... kids. I'm gonna be sick.' And off she charged to join a dozen other spew kinsmen down the back of the boat.

'Where's Mummy gone?' Jaimie repeatedly asked during the rolling voyage.

'Just to the toilet, sweetie. Number two... long time.' The last thing I wanted on my watch was for the kids to think that projectile vomiting was a viable option.

Three hours of pounding seas later, we emerged into the calm protection of the Lofoten Islands. Mandy finally returned and slumped across the table looking pale and wasted.

'Don't worry,' I whispered to her, 'I saved you from the spew embarrassment. I told the kids you were on the toilet.'

'Thanks.'

Jaimie was so relieved to see her again. 'Mummy,' she screamed across the passenger deck for all to hear, 'you must have had a really big poo!'

The island emerged as a massive great silhouette through the blanket of misty rain. It was volcanic, dark and foreboding, as though we were arriving at a dastardly criminal's secret island lair. Towering up out of the sea, sheer-faced cliffs, jagged at their peaks, soared and disappeared into the low clouds. The hulking shadow was sprinkled with the white dots of giant seagulls squawking and diving at the boat.

It was after 9 p.m. and we were completely exhausted from the day's journey. Without pause, I directed us to the campground I had meticulously researched, arriving at the gates to find them locked with a sign reading 'Closed'.

There was a collective groan. I had been too busy working on my shortcut plans to notice that, being the end of August, the short summer camping season was over. 'Oh,' I offered as a brilliant fix-all.

We drove to a cliff top, parked, ate canned beans and crawled into bed. We were cold, hungry and fantasising about hot showers. Mandy in particular wanted to freshen up. During the night another storm whirled in and hit again. The kids started yelling, 'We're scared!' and launched into the hallowed sanctum of our bed, leaving us crushed as we rode Franki's violently swaying motions, wondering if she was going to flip.

'I'm really loving your shortcuts,' Mandy commented in the dark.

In the morning, we drove through engulfing fog to Å. The village was essentially a cluster of colourful red cabins cantilevered on poles out over its small harbour's water. The towering mountain walls we had been mesmerised by the day before remained hidden by the sheath of fog, their presence only betrayed by seagulls squawking from somewhere above. It was a stunning, eerie scene, nothing moved, no boat on the harbour, no person on the streets. The place was a ghost town but one shop was open. I went in, keen to solve our accommodation problem.

'No campgrounds open,' the shopkeeper advised. 'Only *rorbeurs*.'

'Roar whats?'

'*Rorbeurs*.' He pointed to the cabins. 'Old fishing huts,' he explained, 'converted to tourist accommodation. People come from around the world to stay in one. Cheap now, though, it's off season.'

I looked out at the *rorbeurs*. They looked snug and warm. And I liked that word cheap. 'How much?' I asked.

'Forty euros.'

Forty euros! Who did this guy think I was? Howard Hughes? There was no way we could afford such a budget luxury with a year still to go on the road.

I looked across at the van where my family huddled shivering, forlorn and waiting for me to be their hero and return with news of a great campsite with hot showers. They were tired, cold, smelly and sad. We'd been driving twelve hours each day for four days and wild bush camping each night. A day out was desperately needed, so I braced myself and did the only thing I could. 'Sorry, can't afford it.'

I opened the door to a spray of biting wind when he drawled, 'The hot showers will blast your skin like a fire hose. Needs to. For the winter fishermen.'

I stopped and pivoted slowly. 'How hot?'

'Hot.'

I could tell he meant hot hot. 'How much are the tokens for them?'

'Tokens?' The question confused him. 'They're free. You can have as many showers as you want.'

He couldn't have had my forty euros quicker if he'd stuck a gun to my head.

The outlook across the inlet from our *rorbeur* was down to a hundred metres because of the fog and constant drizzling rain. The steep dark cliffs sometimes pushed their foreboding shapes through the mist but otherwise remained shrouded.

A network of timber poles – clothes lines for drying sixteen million cod each year – provided a surreal skeletal addition to the landscape. After turning on the heating, we sat at the table and peered out.

It was 9 a.m. and we now had all day to do nothing. Not a thing. No driving. No planning. No refuelling. We knew where we were sleeping, so no research was required. 'A day off!' I decadently declared. 'This will be like a day spa. Nothing, nothing, nothing!' I lay down at the window and looked out dreamily at the gulls flapping around. Within twenty minutes I was bored.

I started to fidget, unable to do this nothing. Where was the internet when I needed it? We had charged into Europe from Australia and ploughed on up to here. We'd been in constant movement since Amsterdam, rumbling on each day like an unstoppable freight train on a tight timetable. But the greater truth was that we'd been steaming along for months now, maybe years, in our busy life, always with some project, something to do, filling in time like it was an engine needing to be stoked. But stoked for what? More things to do? More business? It was a sickness. I knew it. And I couldn't help it. I was too conditioned from the busy modern world, too far gone, to jump off the speeding freight train.

I gave up, grabbed a pen and started scribbling numbers on a pad, a new project to fill in my time.

'What are you doing?' Mandy asked.

'Sshh! Calculating. Four of us. Twenty-four showers at two euros equals forty-eight euros. That's just under six showers each for us to profit out of staying here.'

I had seven showers that day.

The hut also had another decadence – an oven. Mid-afternoon, I put a chicken in to roast, something we couldn't do in Franki and had missed dearly simply because we couldn't do it in Franki. We poured some wine and the kids played in the attic, its ladder inspiring Jaimie to use her foot again. As the chicken sizzled and filled the rooms with heat and the smell of garlic, the children climbed back down.

In a re-enactment from my bedridden back days, Jaimie stepped forward. 'Do you want to play with us, Daddy?' Callum stood with expectant hope holding Scary Dolly. 'Or,' she reverted to a downcast voice, 'do you have other things to do?'

I dragged my eyes from my book, sat up, took a sip of my wine, smiled and replied, 'Not now, kids, maybe later.'

They accepted that and turned away.

Then I spotted a small white teddy bear. 'Hang on. Who's that?' I pointed.

'Snowy,' Callum replied.

Over the course of the afternoon I was welcomed as a special guest into their world and learnt most of the teddies' names, their favourite colours and preferred food. Together we confronted the dilemma of how many teddies could sit at the dining table for dinner, a prestigious offer akin to being invited to the captain's table on a ship. I suggested the fat ones could sit out but was advised that I wasn't being fair and didn't understand.

Mandy joined in and we were all soon chortling around on the floor between showers. It was different play compared to afternoons and weekend snapshots. Without having to go to work, check email, take a call, or focus on some project of magnified importance, they had my undivided attention and I found myself genuinely enjoying the play, not just pretending for their benefit.

That night both Jaimie and Callum cried out for an escort to take them to the *rorbeur*'s scary foreign toilet. It was very chilly, so I lay still in bed faking sleep, waiting for Mandy to get up. I was a seasoned master at this, a great deception men have successfully hidden from unsuspecting women since time began. The only problem was that my wife was unmoving, comatose, so on this occasion I eventually gave up and shuffled the kids around. In the morning, they told Mandy of these night trips.

'Didn't hear anything, hey sleepy!' I laughed.

She smiled. 'I heard, all right. I was just pretending to be asleep; out-waiting you... for once.'

No one wanted to leave the *rorbeur*, but forty euros a night was an unsustainable extravagance, even with my 'shower-to-profit' matrix calculation.

We spent the following days exploring the archipelago, visiting the villages, driving between the glacier-carved mountains and dressing as Vikings in the world's largest Viking house. As we cruised across the Lofotens and east across the Arctic mainland, we set no nightly destination, covering small distances and stopping wherever we felt the impulse.

At my insistence, we relaxed the no-backtracking rule and detoured a hundred kilometres to visit Sweden's world famous ice hotel in the village of Jukkasjärvi. There was just one small detail I had overlooked. 'To be rebuilt in winter,' the sign read. The ice hotel was a puddle.

'That makes sense, doesn't it,' I observed.

A week earlier this waste of time would have really pissed me off. I might have snapped at Mandy or the kids. Now I stood there slightly bemused. Mandy and I looked at each other and fell down laughing till our stomachs hurt.

The kids weren't too excited about the puddle hotel but there was no controlling them when we arrived at our next stop in Finland.

Santa Claus's village was a Lapland tourist Mecca, but I immediately sensed something was wrong. There should have been hundreds of cars here, even in September.

We tramped over to the famed Arctic Circle post office to find the doors locked, the lights off and a notice in the window. 'Oh my god,' I whispered. It stated that the Santa theme park was closed.

'What does it say, Daddy? What does it saaayyy?'

Mandy was gobsmacked. 'But, but... you... did you actually check if it was open?'

'We-lll. Ummm. Not actually, as in check. Santa makes toys all year round, doesn't he?'

The kids nodded enthusiastically. 'Yeah, Mummy. Santa's elves work all year!'

Santa was a no-show. This would be the worst of all my ill-thought-out broken promises. The lure of the big jolly fellow had been the drawcard that had kept the kids enthralled on our weeks of driving to the Arctic. I would have to resign as Daddy. They would never, ever run into my arms. Missing Legoland was one thing, but seriously, this was Santa! At the North Pole!

I vowed to myself to research and plan everything I would ever do, from now on, forever more, for all eternity, amen.

First, though, I had to man up and deliver this crushing disappointment to the kids. I looked at Mandy, smiled and whimpered, 'Can you tell 'em?'

She backed away as though I was holding a taser gun.

I braced and turned to the kids. Their hopeful little faces looked innocently up at me, unaware I was about to smash them into a pulp with my next words. 'Well, see, ahhh... it's like this...'

The post office door suddenly flung open and a cute Santa elf bounced out. 'You're early!' she chirped. 'Theme park's closed but Santa's grotto opens soon. You guys will be the first.'

I turned back with a grin that would have cracked plaster and spread my arms out wide. 'Surprise! You guys will be the first to see Santa!' My planning vow was instantly forgotten.

Santa sat in the middle of his dark grotto in a glamorous regal chair surrounded by sacks of presents and sparkling fairy lights. 'So little ones!' he boomed. 'Where are you from?'

Callum took one look at this bushy, loud man and clung to his mother like a koala.

'Australia,' Jaimie replied.

'Really?' he roared again in his impossibly deep voice.

I couldn't help grinning like a four-year-old myself. This was no ordinary department store Santa. He had the reddest costume, the whitest beard, the shiniest boots, the crinkliest eyes and a rich, enticing voice so kind I wanted to cuddle into him and tell him everything I'd ever wanted. Instead, I let Jaimie do that.

He then opened up a massive leather-bound atlas to a colourful page showing Australia and asked Jaimie if she wanted to join other children who had neatly written their names within the margins of the beautiful book.

I glanced quickly over at Mandy, knowing Jaimie's writing was suspect. But neither of us intervened quickly enough. Jaimie fist-gripped the pen as though she was about to plunge it into Santa's chest, ignored the book's margins, and etched a giant J from Darwin towards Uluru and continued with more massive letters east across the country.

Santa Claus, the true professional that he was, never flinched. 'Well, well,' he croaked, far more high pitched than before. 'That's... aaahhh... wonderful.'

We scampered out, peeking back to see Santa looking into the tome as though a baby deer had died in the last paragraph.

We had reached the northern apex of our journey, the turnaround point to start our migration south, but on discovering Rovaniemi's beautiful campground set on the banks of the Kemijoki River, complete with a children's playground, we decided to slow down again and declared another day off.

Since our day in the *rorbeur*, it no longer mattered if we wasted a day because it no longer seemed wasted. Without any conscious thought, we had adopted a new natural rhythm: getting up when we woke and going to bed when it was cold. Each day, we'd cruise along, the road east carving through vast fields of tundra with snowy mountains as the distant backdrop. With so few residents living in the Arctic Circle, we were almost always alone. We'd stop for long leisurely breaks, or pouncing on things of interest. The kids forced us to slow down even more, as they became restless with long drives.

We camped wild, building fires, listening to wolves howl at night, resolving to use the camper's toilet on those occasions. Reindeers wandered around our van. Various teddies, on an agreed rotational system, joined us each night for dinner, and these meals became chatty and hilarious. We soon discovered a rich, decadent feeling of timelessness. There was nowhere for us to be. Nowhere to go. No one knew where we were. We had no idea when or where we would arrive, nor did we care. We just kept trundling across the open tundra plains of the Arctic, alone, small and insignificant.

My first job at any new rest spot was to inspect the playground. Since the Fjærland rock-throwing disaster, I had developed skills in identifying rust, glass, splintered wood, broken foot rails, rocks to throw, holes in fences near rivers, stray large wolves – anything that could threaten the kids. There was nothing my eagle eye would miss.

We were also now proficient in our set-up process, a far cry from our bumbling Utrecht arrival. I would scout for a level site to catch the warming sun and get the best view. That established, Mandy and I eased past and around each other like a precision driving team, connecting the power, clicking on the fridge, winding out the awning, unfolding the outdoor furniture, turning on the gas, opening windows, flipping out the stair, plugging in the iPod and chilling the drinks. We'd even developed a sixth sense for the angle of the cupboards and had stopped smashing our heads into them.

As the kids were ensconced in the playground, we added another layer to our slowing down with a 'Big Day Out'. It would be a solo parent sanity break in which one of us would go off on our own to do whatever we wanted. I won the toss and took off on my first 'Johnny time' in weeks, powering out of the campground like a prisoner on a day pass.

My first stop was the library because it had free internet, but after fifteen minutes, this real world intrusion invaded my newfound tranquillity, so I disconnected, no longer wanting or needing that e-buzz.

I returned and tagged with Mandy and later, when she returned, we lay in the sun having an afternoon sleep. But as I was learning from being with the kids constantly, our peace could end at any moment. And it did so in alarming fashion with another piercing scream. After five weeks on the road, I was better attuned to my children's genuine danger tone, and leapt off running, steps ahead of Mandy.

'My foot!' Jaimie was yelling. 'It stings!'

She was hobbling frantically over, looking so frail and in need of me. I crouched down and opened my arms out wide to embrace her into my chest, feeling conflicting guilt that I was happy it was finally me, after all this time, that she was running to. She slowed, looked at me, held her palm up and weaved around me like a footballer avoiding a tackle. 'Not youuu! I want Mummy!'

Cream was applied to a spreading rash before we left her, whimpering, to get Callum. As Mandy walked around the playground, double-checking my prior inspection for the cause of the injury, she stopped and pointed to the bottom of the slide. 'What do you think that is?' she asked in a warning tone that signalled she already knew the answer.

'Weeds?' I guessed in hope.

'Ever heard of stinging nettles?'

'Stinging nettles?' I gasped, before figuring the best form of defence was attack. 'What sort of idiot would put stinging nettles at the bottom of a kids' slide?'

Mandy walked off, glancing back over her shoulder. 'By the way, that playground eagle eye of yours might need some adjusting.'

I stared at the offending greenery and made a mental note to add dangerous plants to the expanding list of 'musts' to check when travelling with small children.

My contributions towards these family dilemmas was proving less than useful, but unfortunately for me, that was about to change. I'd walked out from the Ranua Zoo to find Mandy on the ground next to an open sewerage hole. 'Ah, the joys of emptying the chemical toilet,' I observed.

'Yeah well, I've dropped the bloody cap off the toilet down the hole.'

I peeked cautiously down the hole, glimpsing the cap floating in the brown sludge. 'Oh shit!'

I wasn't trying to be funny.

'Very funny!' she shot back. 'I've been trying to get it out with the awning pole.'

This was a serious dilemma. Without the cap, the toilet would be unusable. On cold bush camping nights when howling wolves were around, when public toilets were unavailable, or for urgent kiddy emergencies, it was a critically valued member of our entourage. Especially now that we had learnt how to drown it with chemicals so it was clean and smelt nice.

'You absolutely have to get it, no matter how,' I declared with Churchill-like gravitas.

'But you're the only one who can reach it,' Mandy replied. 'You'll have to lower yourself down into the hole.'

'Oh. Umm. Well. We don't really need it, do we?'

I eventually accepted my fate, lay on the ground and inched up to the edge of the pit. Mandy lay across my legs as I lowered myself head first into the well. 'Don't let go!' I begged, hoping she had forgotten my recent driving rants at her.

At Briksdalsbreen glacier, we had declared we would support each other more. I just never imagined Mandy having to physically save me from getting in the shit. 'OK, OK, focus! We've got a mission to accomplish,' I cried, as though we were choppering into Nam to rescue a POW.

I began poking around with the awning pole, repeatedly pressing the cap into the wall and dragging it up only to see it fall back down. The smell from the pool of poo below was gagging me, my back and legs straining. After several more attempts I slowly scraped the cap all the way up the wall. Mandy snatched it, causing me to lurch downwards, staring deep into a dark brown future. Slowly I inched back up and was pulled out gasping.

Legendary tales of exploding bowels, projectile vomits and other gross travel experiences fuelled our conversation that night. Had I dropped into the well, we both agreed, I would have been a global finalist for the poo stories' hall of fame, challenging the time Mandy saw a girl flip backwards into a six-foot-high pyramid of faeces in a 'toilet' in India.

This intellectual debate was representative of how we had drifted away over the past weeks from 'normal' conversation topics. We now occupied our days musing on how the kids were like walking landmines, clearing sections of campgrounds the minute child-free campers saw them. Prompted by the occasional sighting of another vehicle, we debated long on why motor home drivers all wave at each other when passing, deciding it was a gesture of affinity, like a cowboy tilting his hat at another gunslinger. The kids joined in our discussions as well, no longer being primarily considered as eating, sleeping, toy-breaking machines, but welcomed as providers of new ideas. All these topics of great import overtook our combined consciousness, throwing into soft focus the shimmering lakes and dense forests we rolled through for days towards Helsinki. Mandy and I had not communicated like this in ages and I could almost feel the bond between us growing closer with every day.

Helsinki was the first significant city we had been in for some time, although the Finnish capital was surprisingly small. It had a compact old town at its centre with beautiful buildings, green parks and cobbled streets. The outdoor café scene was in full swing, filled with tourists that mostly trailed through and down to the port area. The urbanity of the scene, however, was almost intrusive after being in the wilds. I felt the need to get away. Fortunately, the port was filled with giant ferries providing all sorts of unusual options.

On our last night in Scandinavia we were at the dinner table discussing with an array of teddies what they most liked about the meal.

'Snowy likes what you like, Daddy,' Jaimie explained.

I quickly slid my plate of salmon out of Snowy's reach, but was admonished for not understanding his ingrained personal integrity.

What I did understand, however, was that by disconnecting from the world in our Arctic sojourn, we had stopped stoking the engine of time and were finally slowing down the speeding freight train of life. I felt I had discovered the secret pillar of parenthood. Not money, toys or playgrounds. But time.

Unfettered, uncluttered and previously unvalued, time was the foundation from which I was building levels of patience, attention and understanding with my kids that I had never achieved before.

Used well, time offered to make me a better husband and father. It had already made me new friends, like Greeny, Whitey and, of course, Snowy. But could I harness this zen-like mindset? I suspected this state only existed because we were in an unnatural escapist cocoon, that it wasn't transferrable to real life, that I would return home and, faced with work and a list of things to do, I would retreat from this magnificent state of alertness. Even worse, I might backtrack.

Would I be willing to do anything to avoid that? I had ten more months to find out.

6

NO PLACE FOR KIDS

There was no indication that we were on a ship ploughing across the Gulf of Finland or that an ocean existed outside. The 'Fun Club' was a dark cavern, its windows blacked out by thick red velour curtains. Coloured lights reflected off a glittering disco ball which in turn lasered them through hazy smoke and onto mirrored walls. We had entered the room at speed, powering in before realising this was not the highly anticipated children's fun club I had promised.

'Where's the games, Daddy?' Jaimie asked.

'I dunno.' I gripped the kids' hands tight and shuffled across to a grandiose black leather booth. Vegas-style cabaret music was playing. Clusters of big, noisy people clad in leather and fur were packed around a bar, gutturally yelling at each other in a mix of Eastern European dialects, and aggressively jabbing around fat cigars and long stick cigarettes. Everyone was cradling tubs of ale the size of flower vases, swilling them as though the alarm on the *Titanic* had sounded. It may have been early morning on our family-friendly ferry but it was more like a *Saturday Night Fever* gangster party in Gorky Park.

'No place for kids!' Mandy called out.

My eyes focused harder through the haze, zeroing in on a sign above the bar. Beer: two euros. 'No way!' I was at the bar in four strides.

'No place for kids,' was a debate we'd had for days in Helsinki. The direct path to Croatia and the beautiful town of Dubrovnik from the poster on our bathroom wall was through a bunch of Eastern European countries. My vision of them was of some glasnost outpost of poverty and wars. They were reputed to be crime-riddled and dangerous. It was a region where motor homes travelled in convoy for security. Other travellers, who had never been there, warned us not to take the kids.

Yet the enforced remoteness of Scandinavia had been the greatest detoxification programme I could have entered, and like a river changing directions, much of what I had considered logical had altered. I found myself irresistibly drawn to the zinging adventure of a walk-the-plank, jump-into-the-void dare. Like going through the Baltics. But Mandy and I were no longer the independent travellers. Giving in to these mad urges without thought of consequence was a choice that existed before kids. The debate had seesawed for days, but the idea of just leaping off into the great unknown made us feel so alive that reason lost and zing won. We jumped.

The kids thought that all this music, beer, disco lighting, smoking and dancing was the funnest of all fun clubs. I had to agree.

'Will you dance with me, Daddy?' Jaimie asked in her sweetest voice.

I took her for a spin and then encouraged Callum to take over. Jaimie issued him with instructions. They embraced each other like they were hugging trees and began mimicking the dancers. When the other couples spun, the kids spun. Sort of. When they dipped, the kids dipped, kind of, till they fell giggling to the floor. They bumped around like co-joined miniature dodgem cars, bouncing into more serious couples.

'I think they're starting to piss people off,' I observed.

Just then, the music stopped and the dancers broke apart to politely clap. As they did, a crescendo of raucous cheering erupted from the beer-guzzling, chain-smoking mob who were up as one, taking flash photos and whistling at the kids as the two miniature *Fredestaires* recommenced another round of circular hug dancing.

I watched this adulation with a strange envy. 'I was once asked to be a competition ballroom dancer, you know.'

Mandy sprayed a mouthful of gin and tonic across the table. 'You what!' She tried to compute this information from a man she had only ever seen doing white man disco lurching.

'Yeah, but I was too gutless to go out of my comfort zone, to walk the plank.' I nonchalantly shrugged and looked at the kids, admiring how they were too young to have created any such regrets. They'd have a go at anything, even ballroom dancing. I hadn't always done that. There could be few things worse than to die wondering. But at least the Baltic frontier wasn't going to join my list of regrets.

We drove off the ship, confident and unafraid, but this new zeal was quickly undermined once I successfully managed to get us hopelessly lost.

Somewhere in the backwaters of Tallinn, we glided on dirt roads covered with broken glass through a silent wasteland of old concrete buildings, many torn apart, most pockmarked with bullet holes. Clothes were strung out on hundreds of makeshift lines. Battered old cars lay broken. Scrawny dogs snapped at our van. The giant camper cruised on through like a starship from a future world, a beacon of vast wealth worth forty times the average annual income of an Estonian. We were inside my glasnost vision. A group of youths were standing around a fire that was blazing out of a forty-four-gallon drum, watching us intently as though they were preparing to strip Franki down and sell our children for body parts.

I had stuffed up. 'We need to get out of here,' I stated and then stuck my head out the window like a dog.

'What are you doing?' Mandy cried.

'Shush,' I waved back and pointed my thumb at the sky. 'I'm navigating… by the sun!'

'You're what?' she spluttered.

'Haven't you seen *Crocodile Dundee*? I'm trying to find west. This way, absolutely guaranteed,' I pointed.

We were soon at a dead end in a dense forest, somewhere east.

By a dose of extreme navigational fortitude, which I claimed as deliberate genius, we eventually flapped back out onto a main road and deciphered our location.

After this cavalier arrival, I desperately wanted to get my family behind the safety of a nice camping enclosure before dark but when we pulled up the reception looked like a junkyard manager's hut that had taken a mortar hit. To add reassurance, the fences had holes, the grass was long, there was no electricity, and we were advised the site and most others throughout Eastern Europe would close for the summer season on 15 September, in two days' time. Nearby sat another camper, a kindred spirit confirming we weren't mad to be here. It was a battered old Mitsubishi van housing an old, grey-haired, toothless woman who was chatting feverishly to her drooling Alsatian dog.

I decided I needed to do something to improve the situation, so took the kids for a shower. We walked into the toilet block and splashed into a plane of muddy water. I sloshed over to the shower cubicle and pulled back a filthy plastic curtain to find a light bulb hanging on a wire dripping water into a mouldy recess. 'Let's just wash our faces.' At first nothing happened as I screwed hard on the sink taps, but then, as though from the bowels of a monster, a groaning yawn echoed through the building. The pipes started vibrating, the kids started screaming, small paint chips flaked off the walls as though we were in an earthquake, until finally the taps belched and violently spat freezing brown water out all over us. We squealed in unison and sprinted outside. Maybe we shouldn't have jumped.

Day one and we'd lost our nerve. With the camping season shutting down, we decided we had no choice but to charge south to Croatia and treat the Baltics as a transit lane.

Still, we couldn't resist a day visiting Tallinn's renowned fortified old town, a 1,000-year-old enclosure that once had sixty-six towers around its walls. Entering its ramparts, away from the thundering metropolis outside, was like coming out of a snowstorm into a peaceful cottage. The sound of violins led us through cobbled laneways into Raekoja Plats, the town square, lined with beautiful cafés. Restaurant owners were shaking hands with patrons. Waiters with sashes over their arms attended tables. Chefs walked around in big white chef hats. Police passed through in impressive dark uniforms that glistened with ribbons and guns. 'It's like a movie scene,' Mandy observed.

'Yeah. It's gorgeous,' I replied, 'But where's the life? There are no real businesses here. No kids playing ball. No old women knitting in the streets. It's all tea shops and themed Viking dinners. It's very touristy.'

'You're a tourist,' Mandy observed.

'That doesn't mean I want to hang out with other tourists.'

We were glad to escape from the campground's exploding plumbing and the dog-whisperer woman the next day, but an arduous drive focusing on dodging holes, people, carts and animals had us further pondering on the wisdom of our route through the Baltic.

We crossed into Latvia and stopped at the first village we saw so we could collect brochures, having quickly learnt this was the only way to get up-to-date information on open and new campgrounds.

'Planning are you?' Mandy pointedly asked, referring to my fistful of brochures.

I was acutely aware that my penchant for winging it had put my family at unnecessary risk two days earlier. 'Well, we need some structure.'

'Structure?'

'Maybe a bit of planning.' I smiled.

I noticed her hide her own smile.

These brochures led us to Riga City Camping. It was a new site, near the old town and hidden behind a row of industrial sheds. It was essentially a car park, but provided our newly revised list of camping essentials – a security fence and a working power point.

After set-up, I went to inspect the shower block, returning in more rapture than Homer Simpson with a free Duff beer. 'Oh bay-bee!' I announced. 'I have just had possibly the greatest shower... ever... in a public building... on the planet!'

Mandy sprung up as though I had discovered a living dinosaur.

We had given up hope of ever finding a decent shower while camping. To date we had experienced freezing cold water, wet floors, two-minute timers, no water pressure, extra costs for tokens, annoying push buttons to keep the water flowing and nowhere to store clothes while they got soaked. And this was before arriving at Armageddon campground in Tallinn. All these inconveniences were magnified when sharing a cubicle with two small children who screamed incessantly due to any number of these factors. I had only just expelled the words 'hot', 'untimed' and 'free', before Mandy was gone in a trail of whoopee.

Riga's old town felt like a real living beast. Locals were buying everyday things in real shops. Old women were knitting on the streets, my ultimate authenticity barometer. We found a garlic restaurant filled with locals opposite the President's Palace and devoured everything, including the garlic ice cream, but were then unable to breathe near each other for a day. There was also an edge about the place I couldn't quite decipher until Mandy noticed me observing a group of astonishingly beautiful women. 'We're not here so you can buy a Russian bride, you know.'

That clarified the edginess and the groups of bingeing men that dominated the tourist hangouts. Overt billboard advertising was everywhere, enticing men to find brides and browse through girl catalogues. We were in the Slavic bride-buying capital of the world.

We ducked into a tea house and read the English-print tourist paper. 'Wow, listen to this,' I read. 'Beautiful, feminine, sweet, charming, sexy, educated and intelligent women... curious in foreign men. Geez honey, I've already got me one of them.'

Mandy ignored me.

The paper, however, outlined how Latvians were in a dilemma, desperately wanting the tourism cash, but trying to dampen the country's growing reputation as a destination for booze and sex. The rampant advertising standards indicated commercialism was winning over other reform. Maybe they weren't so different from Western governments after all?

I kept reading out loud. 'Many Latvian women feel that marrying a foreigner is the only way to support their families. They have simple aspirations. They are just looking for decent men who are not drunks, liars or jerks.'

Finally I got my wife's attention. She raised her head and smirked. 'They're hopeful.'

We explored more of the old town before taking turns at the Latvian museum of Russian and Nazi occupation, which was definitely no place for kids.

The building was a big grey box, dimly lit inside, creating a dark foreboding mood around its showcases. I shuffled through, immersed in the 1940s, staring deep into the lost faces in the grainy black-and-white images of near-skeletal people being herded onto trains or shot in the streets.

Like kids in a toy box, Russia and Germany had agreed to split up the region rather than fight each other. The Soviets got Finland, Estonia, Latvia and part of Poland. The Germans would get the rest of Poland and most of Lithuania. Once the war started, Latvia was made a Soviet republic and thousands of the population were killed or deported to Siberia. Germany later reneged, invaded Russia and retook Latvia, embarking on a slaughter programme that made the Russians look like a charitable church. By the end of the war, half a million Latvians were dead and this little country was back under the control of the Soviet Union.

Forty years later, in a demonstration called the Baltic Way, two million people across Latvia, Lithuania and Estonia held hands in a 600-mile protest line. Soon after, in 1991, these three states seceded from the Soviet Union.

The citizens of Latvia had had so many liberties taken away but never gave up in their quest for freedom. We witnessed this ongoing fight for survival, driving outside the beautiful tourist façades, in the 'glasnost' backstreets and rural villages. Poverty was rampant, health poor, clean water scarce and prostitution was all too commonplace. Worrying about a bit of cold water in a shower now started to seem a little infantile.

We left Riga the next day on a long meander to the west coast, arriving at dusk at my well-researched campsite – to find it closed. My risk aversion had altered, we would not bush camp. We drove on, finally stumbling across a tattered sign that read 'Beachside camping open'. It didn't promise much, but it was the only offering available. We bumped along a dirt track and out into an open field set behind tree-laden sand dunes. 'Look, two other campers!' I burst out with relief at the protective strength in numbers in this remote outpost. 'More tourists like us!'

'Ah, so now you want to hang around with tourists,' Mandy dryly pointed out.

We inspected the other vehicles' plates, scanning for the prominent single letter that indicated their origin. This had become a game, to see who could call out the most countries. 'F. France!' I pointed at the first van.

'And Germany,' Mandy yelled.

'Ah ha! Wrong! Denmark, stupid. Germany doesn't start with a D!'

'Ever heard of Deutschland, dopey!'

'Oh.'

As we parked, a big bear of a man strutted to our van. 'Me est Horst. You Nederlander?'

'Camper Nederlander!' Mandy poked her chest like Tarzan, 'We Oz-tray-lee-ya!'

That night, howling wind bent the trees and the waves from the Baltic Sea crashed down behind us. Horst lit a fire and called 'Drink?' motioning in the international hand-swilling gesture. We hadn't had a party since leaving Amsterdam. We hadn't even wanted one, happy to hide out in the wild. But I felt a renewed impulse to engage with our life on the road. Horst led off, swinging a large box of red wine and we followed as though he was the Pied Piper and his wine box was the flute.

The French couple joined us. They knew no English but some German. Horst's wife Birgitte spoke some French and English.

Mandy knew some German and I had some basic French. As the night progressed and the children were tucked away, our stilted conversations became more fluent, supercharged each time someone yelled 'Prost!' and Horst would refill our glasses with the dubious but welcome red wine. We soon started speaking in the international language of getting really pissed together, and understood each other far more as the night wore on. With great promises to stay in touch forever, we all eventually rolled into our own campers for the night, knowing we'd never see each other again.

We waved them off the next morning after I had meticulously researched a shortcut to Poland via the Curonian Spit, a narrow strip of Lithuania that slivers out into the Baltic Sea. On arrival at the Curonian Spit, however, I discovered a small impediment to my brilliant plan – Kaliningrad. It was not until I took a good look at our maps that I realised this 220-square-kilometre land mass was a Russian exclave and hence subject to the bureaucratic Russian entry rules. We couldn't take the shortcut without visas, which would cost 480 euros. Missing an entire section of Russia on the map was not my finest navigational moment, but to show my adaptability, I declared an amendment to my travelling policy. 'Backtracking is allowed if it saves a shitload of money.'

With that new guideline established, we found a campground and had just finished setting up when Horst's camper rolled in. The kids squealed with delight and we hugged the Germans as you only do when you see other travellers that you met somewhere before on the road.

Birgitte was missing her grandchildren so insisted parking adjacent to our site, which was very unusual given the force field the children usually exerted on people without kids. 'You go for a walk,' she insisted to Mandy and I.

We glanced at each other like she'd just given us next week's lottery numbers. Mandy and I hadn't had any sans kid time together since we'd touched down in Europe. 'An hour out!' Mandy gasped. 'Just the two of us?'

We paused for a responsibly acceptable moment, then screamed 'We're free!' and tore off like two school kids playing truant.

Horst later cooked a banquet, but of even greater impact was his table setting. 'They have a white tablecloth,' I observed. 'How flash is that!'

A shower, an hour out and now a tablecloth. I was starting to appreciate simple things, particularly in the harsh light of what the people in these countries had endured.

In the morning, we promised to keep in touch with our new friends and this time we even meant it.

Crossing into northern Poland was like changing rooms. The roads instantly deteriorated and we found ourselves in the midst of a swirling tornado of humans, traffic, carts and animals. The navigator within me was on instant alert, speed-learning Polish, interpreting the road signs and confidently issuing fast, accurate instructions for the driver. 'No smashing into people!' I yelled.

Mandy frowned, gripping the wheel in a chokehold.

'Well, that's what the sign says... look!'

The road sign ahead had a circle and diagonal slash similar to a no-smoking symbol, but in this case the slash was crossing out a man getting slammed by a car and rolling up into its windscreen. This seemed odd, but within a few hundred chaotic metres, it was clear that people seemed intent on getting slammed into and rolling up our windscreen.

'Stop the van!' I cried.

'Yes, yes.' Mandy looked at me, trusting I would take action to rescue us from this frenzy. 'What are you going to do?'

'I'm gonna get a photo of that sign!'

The traffic nightmare intensified the next day as we approached the sprawling metropolis of Warsaw. The motorway was heaving with billowing tankers, dilapidated cars, donkey-drawn carts and old tip-trucks overflowing with workers. The going was slow, the smog thick. Mandy was hunched over the wheel in intense concentration. I had maps everywhere, aware that if I missed a turn on the way to our campground we could be swept away for hours.

I missed a turn. We were swept away for hours.

It became somewhat apparent we were lost after our fourth fly-past of the same KFC outlet. 'Why don't you ask for directions?' Mandy suggested.

'Oh come on, that's ridiculous,' I replied. 'Everybody knows men don't ask for directions.'

Mandy stopped and asked a woman for directions and we were at the campground ten minutes later. It was immediately deemed Club Med Warsaw because it was open, had running water from taps that didn't shudder, a working power point and a security guard.

But the greater achievement was that we had not ripped each other's heads off in the traffic chaos. In fact, I was beginning to truly appreciate Mandy's Formula-One driving ability in the cumbersome Franki beast. And so I insisted we celebrate and weaved off across the highway and grabbed a bucket of chicken and two kids' meals... with toys. It was impossible for me to pass Colonel Sanders four times without taking action.

The day after our arrival in Warsaw, we rode an old heaving timber train into the war museum in the city centre, finding a similar tale of atrocity as Latvia's, just with Poland's own story of five million plus deaths. The old town was a compact colourful cluster of buildings, which had been meticulously rebuilt after the originals were destroyed during the war. The main square, a tiny patch of the past, bloomed like a sunflower among the grey lifeless utilitarianism that comprised the rest of the sprawling city's post-war reconstruction.

The Poles may have lost generations of their people but the rebuilding of the old town centre showed they had clearly made a choice that they weren't going to be spiritually defeated by the war. It made me want to see more of the country, to understand more. For the first time since entering the Baltics, we decided to slow down.

On the following Tuesday, I stood looking at a wall covered with discarded crutches, walking sticks and artificial limbs.

The picture known as the Black Madonna dominated the Jasna Góra Monastery at Częstochowa. Legend has it that the Madonna's face bled when thieves tried to steal the painting. This miracle was recognised by the Vatican, and millions of pilgrims travelled to appeal to the Virgin Mary and be healed of physical ailments. The crutches on the wall had been placed there over the centuries by those who had thrown down their supports and walked out.

Throngs of people moved around us, on their knees and in wheelchairs, crying, hugging, grasping rosary beads and genuflecting. It was an overwhelming display of human faith, love and hope.

Days later, hundreds of kilometres away, I stood alone, transfixed by another room filled with discarded crutches, walking sticks and artificial limbs.

This room also included old spectacles, brown suitcases and crumpled black-and-white photos. Another room was filled with hair. More items registered in slow motion as my eyes scanned the piles. Teeth. Children's clothes. Baby's shoes. Personal diaries, some open, revealing the handwriting. I couldn't look away from a raggedy doll with its eye drooping by a thread from the socket. A scary dolly. This was barrack 14, Auschwitz death camp.

I wandered through the camp to the human ovens, before exiting between the two rows of barbed fences and under the metal sign displaying the message *Arbeit Macht Frei*. Work makes you free. Said the spider to the fly.

Mandy and I tagged so she could go in, knowing this was no place for kids. Jaimie and Callum were in the 'cinema room', our bed with the curtains closed, watching cartoons on the laptop. They were laughing and giggling, a surreal soundtrack to the grotesque scene outside.

In that scene – repeated and multiplied in size up the road at Birkenau, Auschwitz II – the grounds were bare, no birds were singing. It was as though all living things sensed a great wickedness had taken place here and stayed away.

I was crippled with incomprehension. How could a rational being get to the point of thinking this was a good idea? I had no personal connection to anyone who had been here. Yet my body had ached with a tangible grief, a guilt. Fifteen thousand camps. Six million Jews. Holocaust. No movie, book or museum could ever do what the power of travel could achieve. None had ever crystallised these numbers into people for me until I saw their handwriting, their hair, until I saw the dolly with the eye hanging out.

Crutches on a wall. Częstochowa. Miracle and hope.

Crutches in a room. Auschwitz. Black tar on my heart. No hope.

Seared like fossils into my soul.

We travelled on to Kraków, deciding to splurge on an apartment for a few nights so we could rest and absorb all this. The one we rented was high up in an old stone building set just behind the Rynek Glowny, Europe's largest medieval town square. We entered the apartment, running through the three tiny rooms as though it were a palace, fawning over the basics we had taken for granted before camping. A bathtub, chairs that didn't fold. The decadence of separate bedrooms.

It was the perfect base from which to explore the medieval city and while the old town seemed busy during the day, Kraków at dusk was like the rapid flowering of a plant. Rynek Glowny and the surrounding streets lit up into a carnival and were flooded with hordes of bohemian students chatting and solving the problems of the world, shopkeepers yelling, musicians and artists playing and painting.

We explored underground bars, discovering rock bands playing to crowds of three in caverns under the square. The kids were warmly welcomed at all venues.

Later we sprang back out into the square and climbed up into a regal horse carriage and set off on a clip-clop journey through a labyrinth of medieval streets and back alleys. Jaimie was beside herself, calling out, 'I feel like a princess!'

I laughed at the animated joy in her face but as we clopped past the site of the Kraków Ghetto, it drew me immediately back to the discarded piles of toys, of the families torn apart and the dolly with the eye hanging loose. I looked at my family, crammed together in this little carriage, certain that I had never appreciated them, or the circumstances of our life, with such a blasting ray of clarity. I had a loving life partner and two healthy kids. We had warm beds, our basics were covered. We could travel, a choice that was unthinkable for the bulk of the planet's population. We could have a cup of water when we wanted it.

Back in the apartment later that night I found a book called *Man's Search for Meaning*. It was written in 1946 by Victor Frankl, an Auschwitz survivor. In it he described how people survived, or didn't survive, in the camps. He detailed how it wasn't always the fittest, the strongest, the smartest or the ones willing to do deals with the guards who survived. One concept resonated strongly with me: that we could have almost everything stripped away, yet we always have the ability to choose our attitude and own way, in any circumstance.

This power of choice was a message that stayed with me, whispering in my ear like a friendly spirit over the following weeks. It made sense to all we had seen, and all we could achieve in the future. Choice.

Over the ensuing weeks, we slashed our way through southern Poland, across the Tatra Mountains and through Slovakia. In Hungary, we rode around on the Budapest trams for two days, admiring the gothic houses of parliament, the string of amazing buildings lining the Danube River, and the art nouveau palace that contained the thermal bathhouse Gellért Füdő. This spa promised relaxing hot springs but after Callum kept yelling, 'Look at the fat man, Daddy!' at a particularly obese nude fellow, we left more stressed than rejuvenated.

These stress levels were peaking on our arrival at the Croatian border.

We had arrived at the Hungarian border days earlier to be confronted with mile-long lines of vehicles. But like a shopper in a supermarket I scanned and found a mysteriously empty lane.

We surged up to the booths, an armed guard squinted out and waved us through.

We laughed at our successful speed entry into Hungary, but stopped giggling three kilometres later when Mandy said, 'N. On the plate. He thought we were EU passport holders.' It appeared we had just illegally entered the country.

Being on the run in Hungary provided the edginess we apparently had wanted, but by the time we approached the Croatian border, it wasn't so cool.

On the way, I had developed a plan to overcome our illegal status. 'Do what I say,' I instructed the kids.

A guard approached and the kids smiled and cried, '*Z'dravo*!' They were so perfectly cute and wonderfully coached; speaking his language was sure to win the guard's heart and keep us out of prison.

'John,' Mandy whispered, 'that's Croatian. We're still in Hungary.'

'Oh!'

'Documents!' he barked.

'*Z'dravo*? Seriously?'

'Stay cool,' I whispered. 'Maybe he can't read them.'

He took our documents and stood there reading them.

He then entered the van, placed his automatic weapon on the kitchen sink, the barrel pointing at my chest, and dropped to his knee. 'Kangaroo!' He patted Callum's head, and then played with Jaimie's doll, turned and walked out.

'Is that it?' Mandy whispered.

We then heard a loud thud, an ancient sound, long dead in this electronic age, but sweet to any traveller. The guard was grandly stamping our passports. Thud! Thud! Thud! We were free again.

'See. No worries.' We were powered by the lure of warmer temperatures and days later discovered a beachside nirvana on the Adriatic Sea in the small Croatian village of Podgora. We were on the cusp of seeing the much-anticipated Dubrovnik, but all of a sudden, felt no desire or need to rush. The campground was ten steps from the water, packed with shady trees and five hundred metres to a promenade that promised fine food from a string of beachfront restaurants. It was the perfect place to declare a holiday from our holiday, yet we found it difficult to switch off. We may have slashed through thousands of kilometres in recent weeks, but the emotional legacy of Poland was harder to leave behind.

We lazed on the beach and the camp chairs. At sunsets, we walked along the promenade to numerous restaurants that served olives, fresh bread, cheese, strips of cured ham and pizzas.

We did this each day, revelling in the knowledge that if we made decisions, any decision, good or bad – not dancing, leaping off into scary countries, eating too much KFC – at least we had the power to choose. And if we stuffed up, so what? We could choose how to react to that. Podgora was a fun diversion but our leap into the Baltics had proven to be inspiring – instilling an iron rod of will that dictated we should not let circumstances, regrets, dream stealers, or the actions of others, tear us down or dictate our happiness. Never again.

On our two final afternoons in Podgora, we witnessed a funeral and a wedding, both processions led by the same accordionist who generally sat on a rock in the ocean each day at sunset. The townsfolk attended both events, just with different coloured veils. The funeral was a solemn march. For the wedding, each business on the promenade set up a table of shot glasses filled with homemade rocket fuel called *rakia*. The procession paused at each one, gulped liquids and moved on. We were dragged out of our chairs and were soon dancing and slamming down cups of petrol and yelling '*Dovidenja!*' which unfortunately I found out later meant 'goodbye' rather than the intended 'cheers'. Jaimie was being swung around by two old women, and Callum was riding in the stroller and being handed treats as we went. Mandy and I were laughing and holding hands. 'Great place for kids!' I said to her, and I was pretty happy to be there.

7

THE POSTER ON THE BATHROOM WALL

It wasn't modern Dubrovnik I ached to see. It was the 'pearl of the Adriatic', the old castle-like fortress that had been depicted on the poster on our bathroom wall. It was the place that had called to me in my suburban home while I shaved and brushed my teeth. It had drawn me forward on the days when I gave in to believing that escaping for a year with my family was utter madness.

From Podgora we wound south down the Adriatic highway, following the line of the sea as the road snaked through lively seaside villages and high up along the cratered coastal mountain side. Along the way, the shimmering turquoise Dalmatian water was our ever-present companion, its plate-glass stillness broken by a sprinkle of islands, cruise ships, fishing boats and ferries.

Locating our campground required no great navigational feat as it was signposted every ten kilometres on the highway leading into Dubrovnik. With that kind of blanket roadside advertising, I guessed correctly that it was government owned, and as such, had a prime hilltop spot in the modern suburbs overlooking the harbour.

On arrival, I was bouncing around like a kid on the day the fair came to town. 'Let's rip in and have a look at the pearl!'

'No, let's wait,' Mandy replied. 'It's been a big drive. Let's go in refreshed tomorrow.'

'Oh, come on. We're only three k's away. The bus'll probably only take five minutes.' I knew she was tempted so kept pushing. 'We won't do much. A quick peek and we'll be back for an afternoon sleep. No worries.'

She agreed but insisted we go after lunch.

I nodded knowingly towards the kids, having come to learn that fuelling them made every outing far more pleasant.

'Look!' Jaimie pointed down to the harbour. 'Three cruise ships, Mummy!'

'I love cruise ships,' I beamed. I was enamoured by everything on this day. 'They're like big modern dinosaurs, just with fairy lights and music.'

We sat on the hilltop, eating sandwiches and swatting clingy feral kittens away before surging off into town.

The streets were choked with traffic. The bus was jam-packed. We stood with our faces wedged into sweaty armpits. Horns blared, car exhaust filtered through. An hour later we were one kilometre from our starting point.

Eventually I glimpsed sight of the towering castle walls. At 1,200 years old and up to twenty-five metres high, they cast a formidable arch over the west gate entrance to the old town. We hauled the kids off the bus and dragged them along. By now, I had realised that my quick trip had clearly not taken into account one thing: our arrival had perfectly coincided with the arrival of 6,000 cruise ship passengers and we were all funnelling towards this one narrow gated entrance.

I was undeterred, grabbing the kids' hands tighter and diving into the flow of people. An English football crowd surging down the street was subdued compared to the commitment of thousands of cruising octogenarians competing to get the best snow globes and crest spoons.

By the time we had shuffled through the outer gate, over the drawbridge and through the inner gate, I felt like part of a herd of cattle going into a dip. The children were terrified and Mandy had a very distinct 'told you so' look on her face. When we eventually burst into the inner compound, there was nothing visible of the renowned Onofrio fountain or the marbled promenade. They were eclipsed by the jostling masses. This was not part of my dream. We wedged over to the side of the main boulevard and leapt into a café. A herd of blazers, boating shoes and coloured hair stampeded past with determined fervour.

'Phew! We're safe in here,' I announced right before more cruisers flooded into the café. I quickly reversed our plan and we took off back out through the Pile gate. It may have been the most beautiful city on the planet, but I hated Dubrovnik.

My appreciation for cruise ships was also strained. That night the kids and I 'barped' our imaginary horns, and like the old movies, waved at the ships as they left port. Now I understood why people wave so joyously when cruisers depart.

I went to bed in a dark mood thinking things could not get worse, but at midnight I was proven wrong. I heard a cup move in the sink, followed soon after by a scurrying sound that seemed like it was under my head.

After our night of free *rakia* at the wedding in Podgora, we had stumbled back to Franki to discover a furry grey mouse scurrying around the floor. At the time, the kids had torn screaming out of the camper as though it was on fire and I had rescued the situation by swashbuckling around with a broom.

'Don't hurt him, he's just a cute little mouse!' Jaimie had yelled.

'Yeah, yeah, chill out! I won't,' I promised. The mouse then darted past my foot and I slammed the end of the broomstick down so hard it would have smashed his skull through to China had I got him. He quickly disappeared but over the next few days poo droppings appeared all over the van and holes had been gnawed into our packaged food. I thought we had lost him on the drive down the coastline but now the mouse was back and his gnawing tortured me for the rest of the night. When I crawled out into the morning sunlight, rubbing my eyes, I just groaned even louder. Two new cruise ships had arrived overnight.

Things may not have been working out the way I wanted, but newly energised with the power of choice, I felt more agile to tack a new direction. 'Right, new plan. There's no need to rush and explore the city in one day. Let's drive north and find a campsite near the ocean.'

'What about the ice cream, Daddy?' Jaimie asked.

'And the sizzling garlic prawns?' Mandy followed.

I had promised these treats to celebrate our Dubrovnik arrival. Were my family delusional? Surely they had worked out by now that my promises were an instant recipe for failure.

We weaved the van back through the harbour district, passing a convoy of coaches stuffed with cruisers. The city was spectacularly backed by a vertical mountain range and we were soon in a slow climb up the highway that ran like a ledge along its side. As in Norway, I relapsed into 'not being in control of the vehicle on cliff edges' phobia and reverted to a hand-clutching sweat. At the same time I was irresistibly drawn to the window as an aerial view of Dubrovnik old town came into view.

'Look at that!' cried Mandy.

'Whooo-ee, what a view!' Then I wondered how she could see backwards towards the view when she was supposed to be looking ahead to keep the van from plunging off the mountain. 'Just drive will you!' I snapped back.

'No, no, look!' she cried again. 'The car. The car!' she screamed. 'Look!'

The serious edge in her tone finally registered. I turned to see her pointing at the temperature gauge. It was on maximum red hot.

Smoke started billowing out of the engine. 'We have to stop!' I cried.

'We can't. We can't stop! We're on a steep slope, the clutch is stuffed and we're in the middle of the highway!'

We spotted the crest of the hill at the same time. 'Up there!'

Mandy ploughed Franki across the road, coming to a grinding halt at a small lookout. I jumped out, ran around and ripped opened the steaming bonnet. Mandy got out and we looked at each other in silent understanding. This was one of our travelling nightmares, breaking down in a non-English speaking country.

'Let it cool,' was my all-knowing strategy. We turned and strolled over to the cliff edge, and there it was in all its glory. Trumpets blared in my head. Before us was an exact picture-perfect replica of the poster on the bathroom wall, except it was real. The white marbled city shimmered like its pearl nickname. Its red clay roofs and medieval spires crunched inside the castle-like walls that dropped vertically into the impossibly still blue waters.

We simultaneously gasped. Our on-ground exploration may have been terrible, but this was like going to a band whose music you have listened to for years and finding to your joy they sound exactly the same live.

'Mummy! Daddeee!'

We'd forgotten the children. I jumped back into Franki and unstrapped them from where they had remained, terrified of the erupting steam.

They may have preferred gelato over historic landmarks, but on this occasion even they gasped. We stood in a line holding hands at the world's greatest lookout, with our broken-down Fiat as the world's most unwelcome backdrop.

After waiting for the engine to cool, I devised a brilliant plan. 'I reckon if we just fill up the radiator, she'll be right.'

Mandy was doubtful of my sudden mechanical expertise so I told her of the time my friends and I had the '73 Lincoln pimpmobile. 'We blew the radiator up in the snow of the Grand Canyon. Admittedly,' I said, 'we probably should have known about antifreeze, but you know, we're from Australia. Anyway, even though the radiator was like someone had fired a shotgun at it, we drove across the States for six weeks, refilling it every four hours.'

This didn't instil her with confidence but she eventually bowed to my insistence. Once Franki was filled and cooled, Mandy was keen to return to the campground to get it looked at there.

'Nah. Let's just crack on. Didn't you listen to my story? It was probably empty. No worries. She'll be right, babe!'

Fifteen minutes later we were down the bottom on the other side of the mountain, further from camp, and I was ripping the top off a steaming engine. 'We may have a bigger leak than I originally envisaged.'

'No kidding... Babe!'

I planned to refill the radiator but discovered the water tanks were empty. It had been my job to fill them back in Podgora but I had been overwhelmed by the *rakia*. After a nap and some card games, I snuck in to a restaurant's yard, grabbed their hose and refilled the tanks. We gave up on the beachfront quest and started the return climb back up the mountain. Three hours later we limped back in to the world's greatest lookout, the motor billowing steam.

We spent another sojourn viewing the city, but rather than worry about the van, had a picnic instead. After all, it was a beautiful day. We later refilled the radiator and drove back down the mountain aware that we needed to make it to camp urgently. We got caught in traffic.

We bunkered down for another engine-cooling vigil as time slipped away. Mandy took the kids for a walk and I sat under a tree, reading a book. Oddly, we were having quite a pleasant day. I hadn't transformed into a ball of frustration. The verbal jousting between Mandy and I had been more fun than fraught. We had made no great conscious decision to be positive in this adversity, it had just come.

While I was waiting, the engine's plume of steam drew attention.

'Do you need some help, sir?'

I looked up to see a bearded chap jumping off his rusted pushbike. I was instantly suspicious of unsolicited help. 'No, thanks, just waiting for it to cool, so we can drive to the campsite and get a mechanic.'

'A mechanic!' he smiled. 'Oh yes! My brother, he is a mechanic.'

I tried not to roll my eyes. Everyone has a brother or cousin who can be whatever is needed at the time.

'Yes, yes,' he said, 'over there!' and pointed down the street to an unsigned workshop. 'Here is my card. Tell him I sent you.' And off he rode.

I looked thoughtfully at his medical practitioner's card, considering the unusual possibility that maybe there was no scam. Curious that a solution may have lobbed in my lap, I hustled over to the mechanic. He could not speak English and my Croatian was limited to *z'dravo* (hello) and *doviđenja* (goodbye), so we mimed. I steered an imaginary wheel and made exploding sounds. He frowned and made a phone call.

The handset was handed over and a voice explained in English some other places I could take the van. There was one. This man's nephew ran the only Fiat workshop in all of Dubrovnik. I was tired and defeated. After seven hours of steaming, filling, steaming and refilling, I needed to be rescued.

'A tow truck?' Mandy asked when I returned. 'How much is that going to cost?'

'I dunno.' I was somewhat reputed for manic bartering so this reply shocked her more than my calm acceptance of the situation. 'Do we have a choice?'

Ninety minutes later, the four of us were crammed in the front of a large tow truck with a hairy driver who looked like

Bigfoot in blue overalls. Franki was strapped to the back and we soon passed the poster viewpoint for the third time that day. I looked forlornly back at the city, realising my long fantasised visit might never happen.

Our second night in this destination of my dreams was spent in the rear of a mechanic's workshop parked over an open grease pit. As we bunkered down to sleep, Jaimie squeaked from behind her curtain, 'Daddy?'

'Yeah?'

'I thought you promised we were having ice cream tonight?'

The next morning we were given the dreadful news. The radiator, clutch and a bevy of other bits that made the van go round were busted: 1,000 euros. Two days to fly the parts in from Zagreb. This was budget-crushing. Weeks of living expenses would be wiped out. After I mentally regrouped, the mechanic suggested we could sleep in the van while it was on blocks over the oil pit. I instantly accepted, calculating that we needed to stay over that pit for fifty nights to recoup our money.

Three days of sitting in a field attempting to master Sudoku while the kids chased cats was enough. Each day we were told the parts would arrive tomorrow, but each tomorrow brought another reason that delayed their arrival. It was again time to take charge.

Cavtat was the nearest village, ten kilometres south of Dubrovnik and set around a beautiful small harbour lined with stone buildings and filled with sailing craft. There was a beach, masquerading as a patch of stones, to jump off into the crystal clear waters. One visit and we decided to upgrade from the workshop pit before we overdosed on oil vapours.

For twenty euros per night, we moved into a one-bedroom apartment on the hilltop high above the village, bursting into the tiny apartment as though it were the Ritz. I hugged the fridge like it was a slightly oversized lover and let its coolness caress me. We blasted ourselves in the shower and flicked away at the TV channels.

We settled quickly into Cavtat life, buying fresh supplies from the local shop, listening to the church bells bonging, swimming in the harbour, drinking coffee and wine, and nibbling on pizza, seafood, cheese, olives and smoked hams. Each day, Mandy or I would catch the bus to the workshop to reconfirm the parts were expected 'tomorrow', and each day we cared less about the parts or the cost, just going with the flow. We had originally aimed to get an apartment in Dubrovnik and live the Croat life. We were doing just that, with Cavtat being the unwanted accident we came to adore.

We thought the kids were also loving our nomadic time together, but after a week in this little village, Callum dropped a bomb. 'When are we going home, Mummy?' He still took all serious dilemmas to his mum, much to my chagrin.

I held my breath in a sharp intake at the question. This was the moment we had discussed and feared. Many people had warned us the children would eventually get bored on the road. The kids had mentioned missing their friends and cousins a few times, but it seemed the comforts of the Cavtat apartment, with its TV and running hot water, had reminded them even more of the material luxuries of home life. We knew that without their engagement our year away would become a constant arm wrestle. Mandy and I shot glances at each other.

'We-llll,' Mandy drawled in thought, 'we've still got lots of places to go.' She then prattled on nervously, selling him and an attentive Jaimie on the concept of ongoing travel and all the great things they would see and do. She talked of exotic beaches and castles and swing sets and gelato, and finished in a flurry, speaking like a hyped-up *Sesame Street* presenter. 'And when we eventually get home, you'll have your own bedrooms again, with the toy cars and fairies on the bedspreads and lots of things to play with and bikes to ride.'

The two children sat in silence, glancing at each other and slowly digesting this bounty of information. I too sat in silence, scanning their reaction with hidden intensity.

Callum finally looked up. 'Yes, but when are we going home, Mummy? When are we going back to Franki?'

Mandy and I were caught frozen in a long, shocked pause, then looked at each other and burst out laughing. 'You are so right, matey!' I grabbed him up. 'Our home is wherever we are... together.'

It took Callum's innocent question to remind me that home was about the people, how they connected and cared for each other, not some designated pile of bricks and mortar with new couches and the latest flat screen TV.

His question was answered when Franki's parts finally arrived and we returned to our home on wheels.

Mandy's friend Chrissie flew in the same day, delivering on her promise in Amsterdam to meet us here. We were eagerly looking forward to having another adult to play with and took off to explore the islands north of Dubrovnik.

Chrissie slept on the kitchen table, which Mandy had repaired after the Norway collapse. For the first two nights we all slept well, until the mouse, which had somehow evaded eviction in the workshop, recommenced his night-time scratching.

I couldn't bear any more gnawing sleepless nights. I charged off to a supermarket looking for mouse-killing machines, explaining what I wanted to the shop assistants in my now proficient Croatian. They brought me fly swats, cleaning goods and tampons. To get the message across, I reluctantly put my hands up like paws, scrunched my nose, stuck out my teeth and squeaked at them. I eventually left with my hands full of rat glue and the shop assistants waving farewell by sticking their tongues out and pretending to be dead.

'How did you go?' Mandy asked. She and I had been competing for weeks about who was most adept at speaking the various foreign languages, taking great joy when the other made a fool of themselves.

'Yeah, no worries. They knew exactly what I was talking about.'

I read the instructions for the glue with more attention than I'd paid to any campsite brochure or road map. I then carefully poured the glue onto cardboard pieces and stuck cheese chunks in the middle. The plan was that the gluttonous idiot would come out, get stuck, and I would release him.

'Humane. Very good,' Mandy and Chris agreed. I personally would have been happy to pump the mouse full of holes from a shotgun.

Upon inspection the following morning, I saw immediately that the cheese was gone, but my prisoner was nowhere to be seen. I stepped forward to investigate and squelched into a puddle of the clear liquid glue. It had flowed off the cardboard and over the floor during the night because the van was on a slight tilt. I cursed and sprayed insults, yanking my foot up as though it was stuck on cheesy pizza. The mouse was gone and I was the idiot stuck in the glue.

Later that day, Chris announced, 'I have to visit Vladka,' explaining that on each visit to Croatia she always went to see her father's pre-war girlfriend. 'Do you want to come? I think you will find it interesting.'

Vladka lived in a beautiful old vine-covered stone house overlooking the water at Lopud, just north of Dubrovnik. She treated us to a flamboyant double-cheek-kissing entrance, and then led us through a myriad of dark curtained rooms and furniture draped with sheets. Most of the house had not been used in years, but the kitchen was bathed in bright light.

Vladka was like a grand dame of the opera. Every move she made, every inflection in her voice, was theatrically dramatic and we were her audience for the day. Her eyes sparkled with youth when she began filling the room with stories of war and love and dancing from the 1930s, but her mind often changed directions quickly.

'Where are you staying in Croatia?' she asked.

Chris stiffened in the chair next to me.

'Oh, we are camping,' I replied enthusiastically.

Vladka froze and darted a glance at Chris who was sitting there like a child caught with her hand in the cookie jar. 'Kamping!' she spat the K out as though coughing up a fur ball. 'Oh, how utterly ghastly! I couldn't think of anything worse... and with those two?' She stabbed a finger at our crumb-covered children who were presenting a convincing argument as to why you wouldn't camp with them.

She continued to mesmerise us with even richer, longer yesteryear stories that ebbed and flowed through a rollercoaster of emotions. At one stage she paused in her telling and gazed in silence at Jaimie. I leant forward, wondering what amazing memory had been induced by the sight of my pretty daughter. 'Oh what a shame the little girl's hair is not brushed,' she said sadly.

It occurred to me later that the house was a manifestation of her life. Three-quarters in the past, a small part in the bright light of now. The best days of her life were rich, exciting and gone.

I pondered on this for some days and rewound bright chunks of my life that stood out – adventurous, outrageous times when my friends and I strutted the world, ten feet tall and bulletproof, back when we were kings. After my back snapped and my job went poof, I discovered just how easy it was to fall into the trap of looking back at the 'king' times and believing they could never be repeated. And then to wonder, *is this it?*

The secret, I realised after the Vladka visit, was to continually invent the next 'When we are kings' times. To keep leaping off the plank into stupid, crazy shit.

As we rounded the headland to Dubrovnik later that afternoon, I realised happily that I was already doing that.

We had finally made it back to Dubrovnik and rented a two-bedroom apartment in the modern suburb of Lapad. On the first morning I sat on the deck and observed there were no cruise ships in harbour. This was a call to action, so I shook everyone awake.

We clambered onto the same bus we had ridden weeks earlier, arrived at the city gates within minutes and walked peacefully through the stone arches. And that was it. No trumpets. No sirens. I was finally inside the poster on the bathroom wall.

We walked the city ramparts and through the labyrinth of alleys that crept up the mountain on one side of the marble mile and flattened towards the seawall on the other. In odd spots, among beautiful villas, war-torn buildings from the Bosnian War in the early nineties still lay shattered and in rubble, or partly rebuilt, with bright red roof tiles replacing the century-old, deep red ones. We visited the aquarium set inside the harbour wall and later nestled in a quaint little restaurant up a narrow cobbled alleyway where we ate sizzling garlic prawns and ice cream.

After Chrissie left and another friend, Sue, arrived, we continued exploring the city on cruiser-free days and discovered more hidden cafés clinging to the outer walls over the sea – great boisterous places for cheap local food and music-laden nights. Without the tourist hordes, it was like being inside Disneyland after it's closed. Dubrovnik had finally won me over.

When we finally left Croatia and caught the ferry across the Adriatic Sea from Split to Ancona, it was a perfect starry night. I was up on the roof deck alone, and for the first time on the trip, had no idea where we were going. We had no plans, no time constraints, and could go wherever we wanted. Europe was our oyster. And as that knowledge and uncertainty dawned, I was overwhelmed by a sensation of complete and utter freedom that led me to do the only thing possible when feeling so alive while standing at the front of a big boat. I had thrown my arms out wide and screamed, 'I'm king of the world!'

I knew, though, that the challenge to constantly invent more 'king' times promised to be an ever greater quest. My search began in earnest now, accompanied by my wife, two kids and one furry little mouse.

8

THE TRAVEL ZONE

We soon understood why Napoleon had once called Venice's Piazza San Marco the drawing room of Europe. St Mark's Basilica dominated the scene, ably supported by the campanile with its five bells in the tower, the Doge's Palace and the grand Roman columns lining the square. They all combined to guarantee the rapture of the most heathen of travellers. Even the children stood in the square, tense and uncharacteristically alert. I was pleased to witness their reverence. Finally their gelato-focused minds were appreciating the majestic cultural treats on this journey. I turned to see what amazing feature they were so intensely absorbing, just as they swayed back and ploughed off into a sea of pigeons.

It was an entertaining day, sitting in the square, drinking coffee, people-watching and tormenting birds. Venice was stuffed with hordes of tourists – 60,000 a day – all trekking to the must-see sights: Peggy Guggenheim's house, the royal opera house, gondola rides, glass-blowing tours, Casanova's prison cell and the world's first Jewish ghetto.

My wife, like my children, had other priorities. 'I want to get my hair done.'

'In V-V-Venice?' I saw our daily budget going up in a flame of hair rinses. 'Pretty expensive... in Venice!' I said again, applying the 'repeat louder' principle that would ensure she would wilt from such madness.

'That's exactly why!' she emphasised. 'It's Venice!'

With that sort of logic I should have been playing golf at Augusta.

'Why don't I just do it with the clippers?' I had become the family barber since being on the road. Admittedly Mandy's hair was starting to take on a chunky, hacked look, but it was cheap. I had long ago stopped enquiring about the cost of my wife's hairdressing as it often led to more uncomfortable questions like, 'How much did you spend on golf last month?' so I wisely said nothing as she bounced off the next day.

When she returned I fortunately remembered why she was gone. 'Looks fabulous,' I complimented. 'Well worth it,' I added, taking false sincerity to an Olympic level.

The fact was I couldn't see much difference. All I know is that the male of the human species, who are constantly reprimanded for our lack of observance of small details ('How could you not see the pile of clothes on the floor?'), are expected to have an uncanny ability to detect the details of a fine hair adjustment. And if a man pulls off that minor miracle and feigns a response about how his partner looks so much more beautiful than before, he is then grilled as to whether he thought she looked like shit previously. It's a complete recipe for disaster, second only to the unforgivable sin of pausing before replying to any question revolving around the size of her bum.

We would never discuss the cost. Mandy would be happy I didn't ask and I would pretend the euro amount didn't jump off the bank statement at me like an attacking monkey.

That night, Camping Fusina's bar was heaving with backpackers and we teamed up with another Aussie family, which was like discovering a kindred smoker at a party. Tommy and Michelle were motor-homing around Europe while being simultaneously tortured by their teenage son. His protest over being forcibly kidnapped from his friends to go on a world tour included being constantly wired to his iPod, and getting his hair dyed bright orange. This was one haircut other males noticed.

For many driving days Mandy and I entertained ourselves with an ongoing debate about the 'winner' items on this trip – the things that we couldn't do without. The finalists were eventually decided as the iPod, the double stroller (ideal for narrow streets and for the kids to sleep in at restaurants), the laptop for digital photos and DVDs, a flotilla of teddies, the camper toilet (with fresh chemicals), and wine glasses kept constantly chilled.

The kids added their own favourites that included the drawing of circles, playgrounds, chips, tea parties, beaches, counting church bells, carrots and gelato ice cream. Carrots? What was with that? I would listen to them chatting away like two chipmunks planning a nest, getting a unique insight into how their little minds ticked. One discovery was that Jaimie would often tell Callum that if something was really good, it was only for girls. This seemed to have no boundaries and could include the song he was singing, the toy he was playing with or even the shower cubicle he was in. At age two, he generally accepted her wisdom, but signs of resistance were emerging. One evening, Callum sidled up to me. 'Daddy?' he whispered.

'Yes, son?'

'Jaimie said my clothes are silly.'

I froze. Until now, all his major life issues had been addressed to his mother, and this was our first ever Cat Stevens father and son moment. I instantly recalled my dreams of fatherhood in which I had imagined being a wise oracle for my children, dispersing sage advice like Yoda to Luke Skywalker. Now the chance to establish myself as his champion and break the mother bond had arrived. I smiled, looked into his eyes, and, zap, I had nothing. My mind went blank. 'We-e-ellll!' I drawled, buying time. 'So… ummm, you don't like that?' Spectacular! I was repeating questions back like a cheap psychiatrist.

'No!'

'Wee-elll.' More brain-scanning. The only thing I could think of was that I had dressed him and, yes, he did look a little silly. But I knew I must not laugh at his concerns or he might never confide in me again. 'Should I tell her to… umm… maybe, stop saying that?'

'Yes,' he spat.

Excellent, a solution! Constantly spending time with my kids had finally paid off. Daddy of the Year award coming my way. I was on a roll, so I wrapped an arm around him. 'You know what, mate? One day you're going to be pretty happy that girls are checking you out.' He recoiled in shock, so I rushed on. 'Well, not your sister, of course. I mean, that would be... sorta weird... I suppose. But other girls. You know... umm, cute ones... umm, girlfriends. Ones you might kiss.'

'Maaaarrr-meeee!'

Our close-knit camper life had the strange effect of magnifying this and every other event. Days later Callum strutted up to us after dinner outside the camper and declared, 'I ate my beans!'

Mandy and I both leapt up. At every meal, for two years without fail, we had put vegetables on Callum's plate. For two years, he had never eaten one. We kept placing them there, hiding them, disguising them. He kept ignoring them. With the delivery of this momentous news, we scanned his plate and under the table as though we were looking for a diamond that had fallen out of a ring. But it was true, he'd eaten a vegetable. This achievement would have once gone unnoticed in our time-poor, inattentive existence, but now we whooped and hollered and spun him around, dancing under the stars singing, 'I ate my bean' to the tune of ABBA's 'Dancing Queen'. 'Crisp and green... like a tambourine, yeah yeah!' The lyrics may have needed some work, but in the history of the world, never had the eating of a bean been so celebrated.

The 'day of the bean', however, highlighted other 'insignificant' achievements I had missed, like the kids' first steps and their first words. Being wholly present, in both mind and body, was uncovering some secret joys of parenthood that I didn't know about or expect to care about. It made me wonder how I could make sure I was there in the future for their first catch, first lost tooth, and first day at school. Imagine the singing associated with Callum's first piece of broccoli! This line of thinking raised so many unanswered questions, like what ABBA song lyrics rhyme with broccoli?

I continued working on this linguistic puzzle as we journeyed across northern Italy, my mind also drifting off into other wild and wonderful thoughts, prompted by whatever was happening at the time. Without email, phone calls, work and other Venus flytraps of time and brain span, I was acutely focused on nothing but the immediate activity. It was while I was in this mode that we arrived in Turin.

Luca and Marina were friends we had known for years. Mandy had met them in the tropical rainforests of far north Australia while on a reef-diving expedition. They lived in a beautiful loft apartment in Turin's old town with their three-year-old son Guglielmo. We stored Franki in a nearby campground and moved in to their spare room, quickly falling out of camping mode and into the wonderful ease of domesticity in which showers were untimed and toilets miraculously emptied themselves. The children in particular embraced these comforts once they discovered Guglielmo's veritable department store of toys when compared to their one small plastic box of possessions in Franki. And so, while Luca was immersed in his management role and Marina worked from home PR consulting, we played.

With so much unbound time, I seemed to have discovered a sensory superpower, seeing rapture and poignancy in every transaction, noticing things I never would have when previously hurtling through life's daily activities. It was as though the smell and colour of flowers had intensified. I would hear a violinist from hundreds of metres away and lead the family through the streets to sit and listen. The kids, too, were rapt. Separated from computers and TV, they seemed to have taken on an attention span beyond their age. Hours could slide by like minutes as we listened to a bird tweet or watched a guy make a pizza. I observed our friends' daily routines from a curious distance. Luca would arrive home after work late each night while Marina juggled her own job and Gugli's needs. What gripped me was that their lifestyle mirrored our recent former life, and exposed it as the complete opposite of the magic zone we had fallen into.

It seemed as though in our thirties we become responsible because having big debts and crying babies is serious. We further complicate things by clamping on balls and chains to our aspirations and freedom in the form of big loans for unneeded 'things'. And then we row hard in the bowels of the slave ship, doing lots of stuff we don't want to, dreaming of the day when we can afford to do what we really want. And when that day comes we wonder why we didn't wake up to the fact that life is short and that we should have chased our real dreams earlier.

We, too, had a mortgage and kids who needed schooling and food. But after months on the road, my mind was fracturing. I started to wonder. Could we change our entrenched ways? Chase rainbows while we could still run? Work at things we love? How much of our life must we spend climbing the hill before letting the handbrake off and freewheeling down with gay abandon? A voice in my head kept whispering, like a sinister hiss in a tunnel, that one good job offer, one too many bills and this unearthly feeling of hope and opportunity could crumble like the pillars of Rome.

I decided we needed to get back on the road. Travel may initially have been a convenient escape from reality, but it was now the one place free of distractions where we could flow in a kind of effortless serenity.

After crossing the Italian Alps, catching colds in Monaco and hitting snow in the Pyrenees, we travelled to Barcelona for some warmth. On the long drive down from Andorra I kept the family spirits up by raving about the magnificent waterfront campsites ahead, but on arrival found them all flooded and closed. My beachfront extravaganza was yet another shattered ill-formed promise. I was starting to think I had the makings of a career politician.

On this occasion, however, instead of navigating around for an hour insisting I knew where to go, I decided to ask for assistance, directing Mandy to drive over to a line of girls who were sitting roadside in plastic chairs and waving at us. I wound down the window, leant out and asked the closest lady, in my mangled attempt at Spanish, if she knew where something might be open. *'Donde este un place ouvre por favor?'*

The girl grinned, flicked her hair back and slowly spread her legs wide apart, revealing, for even the most inattentive of observers, that she was wearing no underwear. Mandy roared Franki off down the highway past the line of prostitutes before I could investigate further.

'Did she show you where something was open?' Jaimie called from the back.

'Oh yeah. She did that all right!'

We eventually found accommodation that was open. Camping Villanova had over 1,500 sites. We had deliberately avoided these super camps as they were promoted as family budget mini-resorts, but sounded more like zoo enclosures stuffed with screaming children. Not that I disliked children, in fact I really liked my own. I just didn't want to camp as though we were living inside Disney's Space Mountain.

'Tomorrow we'll find somewhere better,' I said.

'But why would we leave, Daddy?' Jaimie asked.

I was adamant that no self-respecting traveller would be seen dead here. People come to these bubbles and stayed for weeks, speaking English with expats, guzzling beer and playing board games. They never even walked out the front gate!

After setting up, I announced I would, 'Reccy this bourgeois enclave!' My habitual first inspection, the litmus test of campsite quality, was the toilets. They were sparkling clean and filled with items never before seen in a camping facility – toilet paper and shampoo dispensers. I strolled further through the grounds. There were swimming pools, playgrounds, tennis courts, a restaurant, two bars, an internet café, a supermarket, indoor heated pool, spa, a serviced laundry, and vehicle detailing bays. There was regular live music, kids' parties, a child-minding service, an animal petting zoo, barbecues, daily English newspaper delivery to the van, and an automatic ice cream dispenser. For eighteen euros per night.

We stayed six days, speaking English with expats, guzzling beer and playing board games. We didn't walk out the front gates once.

During this layover, we read, chatted, cooked, played games and wrote long fanciful letters home to my mother, known to the kids as Nana. I was also able to give undivided attention to the eradication of the mouse. His ongoing presence since

Croatia had become pure torture, his nightly scuffling leaving us cranky with sleeplessness, eclipsing the initiation pains we had when first squeezing into Franki. Brooms, cats, poisonous meat and pellets: every plan I'd developed had failed. I was starting to feel as though I was being constantly outwitted by a superior intellect. But after weeks of taste-testing cheese bait, stepping in rat glue and making mouse noises with an array of shopkeepers across Europe, I had finally become as one with the mouse. To catch a mouse, I decided, I must think like a mouse.

In doing so, I spent another sleepless night developing a plan. 'We have to put ourselves in his shoes, or paws,' I said to Mandy with the gravitas of a flying squad leader who knows he doesn't have enough fuel to return. 'If we tape up a series of garbage bags, then spring a surprise on his nest under our mattress, and mace him in the face, he will jump over the front of the bed. That's what I would do if I were him.'

Mandy gave her sleep-deprived, wild-eyed consent and we spent hours blocking all possible escape trajectories. Finally, prepared, I counted three fingers off as though we were about to jump out of a foxhole and run into a shower of bullets. 'Go!' I yelled.

Mandy ripped up the mattress and there he sat, quivering and cute with little wet brown eyes. I was gripped with guilt for a moment, rodent Stockholm syndrome, but snapped out fast and started macing and screeching. The little mouse scampered around until eventually, trapped, he turned, looked into my eyes, ran and launched at me. I stumbled backwards, certain this super mouse could now fly, but he slowly arched down into garbage bag number three, having not anticipated my brilliant bag strategy.

Mandy bolted off and released him a kilometre away.

Our camping neighbours from the north of England had been watching our escapades with some amusement. 'I 'ope you took 'im a loong way away,' sailed a thick accent over the hedge.

'He can come back?' I asked in terror.

'Aye, lad.' The man sounded like a publican warning me of werewolves on the moors. 'They can smell their way back to their nests.'

I couldn't sleep all night anticipating his return. I put milk outside for the camp cats. I knew his inner thoughts. Somewhere in a grassy field he was traipsing his way back. We decided to leave Villanova at dawn, to go far, far away.

Our travels sans mouse took on a semblance of normality. We ate. We slept. We read, shopped, showered and cooked. We bought petrol and bread and swept the floors. We bush camped for free. We picnicked. Each afternoon, we got the maps out and devised a new route, often detouring at whim for anything of interest. We had lost all desire to traipse around the heralded must-sees.

In northern Spain, in Bilbao's old quarter, the Casco Viejo, we even discovered the secret to daytime entertainment – lunch. The tapas bar we chose after a morning at the Guggenheim had been filled with people plunging into wine, cigarettes and plates of goat's cheese and calamari. I liked it immediately. There was something deliciously naughty about heavy smoking in a place of food. And in these places, the children were often spirited away and fawned over by other patrons while we were plied with more food and wine than we could possibly devour.

Our days were full of a lot of ordinary things.

I was beginning to recognise how extraordinary this ordinariness was.

We'd arrived in Lagos, a little coastal village down the bottom of Portugal near Europe's most south-westerly point, in early December with the theory of holing up for winter. Like many of my well-laid plans, it was quickly thwarted when we found the town's campsite was closed. This led to the discovery of the mythical phenomenon of the official/unofficial European campsite.

Across the river from the town centre was such a place, where campers clustered together in a sort of rolling neighbourhood watch. It was impossible to ignore the large municipal 'No Camping' sign dominating the site, but a robust German woman with two obese cats insisted we could either stay here for free or go in to the local supermarket car park after close and leave early in the morning. The ideal winter getaway I had imagined did not include illegal squatting or sneaking in and out of bitumen car parks under cover of dark. I looked around at these rigs worth 40–60,000 euros, curious that their owners were so tight they would rather save fifteen quid by camping on a dirt pad than pay a few shekels for a nice campsite.

'Hold on,' I asked the German cat lady, 'did you say… free?'

'Ooh, ya. Of course.'

Our deck chairs were out within minutes.

Lagos was architecturally beautiful. Whitewashed buildings, red tile roofs, cobbled lanes and the odd donkey. But it was also drowning in English package holidaymakers. A replica

English pub lined with Union Jacks was loudly pumping out Oasis and the Rolling Stones. Estate agencies advertised villas in English pounds. The *Daily Mail, The Sun* and *The Times* were on news-stands. Signs advertised 'real' English breakfasts of bacon, eggs, sausages, fried mushroom, tomatoes, baked beans, chips, toast and milky tea. Waiters wore English football jerseys. Churrasquera, the infamous Portuguese spicy grilled chicken, was off the menu replaced by bangers and mash.

'I travel to immerse myself in the local culture,' I pontificated that night. 'You know, to speak the lingo, listen to the music and meet the people. These tourists are parasites on the local culture!' With that declaration, I went back to reading the imported *Daily Mail*, listening to Billy Bragg and squatting in the illegal campsite on Portuguese public land.

The view across Lagos' Bensafrim River each evening was dominated by a line of Christmas trees lit up with thousands of fairy lights. It was a good place to reflect on three chance meetings we had had in the previous weeks – the axis of discovery, I called them.

One was outside Carrapateira in southern Portugal, at a surf beach Mecca, the Praia do Amado, that was described as being home to a controversial but low-key community of travellers. I was drawn there by the word 'controversial', but on arrival, our motoring beast, for once, looked very middle class among a cluster of battered technicoloured campers. We were reassured by the presence of another family, although with their four straggly kids clad in brand name surf wear, they were well in the scene. They'd chucked their jobs and the whole family was sleeping on one big mattress in the back of their kombi. Chasing waves around Europe and Morocco was their dream and that's what they were doing.

We sat on the cliff top that night among the surfer dudes, watching line after line of glorious waves pump into the cove, and joined in making a sizzling 'Sssssst' sound as the perfect orange sun dipped into the Atlantic. The father described to me how many people told him he was mad to go off and travel like this, but then he smiled and said, 'Fuck it, man. Just 'cause we have kids doesn't mean we have to put our own life on hold.'

I wanted to hug him, but that would have been inappropriate given I had just met him and didn't find him overly attractive. For months now we had met people pursuing their passions. No one had asked us what we 'did'. No working occupation defined our worth. Being on the road, among kindred travellers and wave hunters, was the most centred I had felt in years.

The second discovery was in meeting an English family who had sold their home and were criss-crossing the continent for two years while correspondence schooling their five daughters, aged five to fourteen, on the way. 'We've become so much closer as a family,' Fran, the mother told us. 'It was painful at the start, all over each other.' I knew what she meant. 'But now we can't imagine a better way to live. Bryce and the girls are getting on like they never had before. As a family we used to argue and spend no time together. Now, this caravanning life, free of all the trappings, it's like we have given ourselves this gift. We've just entered a new zone.'

This was a find. 'This zone she's talking about,' I later declared, 'is the great gift of travel! The reason for travel! The magnificent attentiveness, the losing of yourself in the simplest of activities. We can't truly shine when we fill up every moment with something to do. You can't achieve this sort of mind release when squeezing in a few weeks of holiday each year. Half that time is spent de-stressing, and with mobile devices and phones, we never really escape.'

But it wasn't till the third chance meeting that I sensed what being in the travel zone could lead to. We had met an old man outside a tenth-century Benedictine abbey at Santa Domingo de Silos, a small village hidden away in the rolling hills of central north Spain. He was an unlikely looking conveyor of great wisdom, hunched over with bulging eyes that looked like bloodshot cue balls. We'd gone there to hear the Gregorian chants of the monks, famed for their singing on the Enigma CD. Resplendent in their orange robes, they had shuffled silently through the cold stark church, bewitching us with their chants and transporting us back to another time. But it was the old man who provided the greater light. He told us he was on a pilgrimage.

'To where?' I had asked.

'Compostela, of course.' He detected my ignorance, so clarified. 'The Camino de Santiago de Compostela,' he stated in that irresistibly rich Spanish-accented English that sounded like Antonio Banderas.

As legend goes, Saint James the apostle had his head chopped off by Herod in 44 AD and was later buried on the far north coast of Spain. A hermit rediscovered his mausoleum in 813, and a cathedral and town was built over and around it. By 1000 AD, the 450-mile trek to worship at his gravesite, which passed through fields and villages along the Camino de Santiago, had become the greatest route of pilgrimage in the Christian world.

We criss-crossed 'the way of St James' over the following week, eventually standing at the Camino's end point, the cathedral, a great ancient structure that stood like a furrowed old giant over Compostela's thriving inner walled city. Inside, unshaven, weary travellers shuffled around, many carrying long poles and dressed in garb replicating ancient times. Many had been on the road for months. Some were hugging, crying or praying, others lining up to embrace St James' statue and climb down into his gold-glittering crypt under the temple. The old pilgrim had told us about this. 'It is a spiritual journey,' he had said. 'Not just one of challenging travel. It is more about personal transformation. With time out and reflection over many months, we will often return changed from the person we were when we began.'

With Mandy and I prompting him on, he whispered of 'a boon', as though he were imparting details of where the Ark of the Covenant was hidden. 'A revelation, maybe a change of beliefs, but really, something in here.' He tapped his skull. 'We will see all the familiar things when we return home, but we will see them through new eyes.'

I was already aware of how my mind had been drifting from the pier of entrenched beliefs over the trip, but now recognised that in escaping from 'normality', and spending many months of disconnecting to get into the travel zone, we were strapped in for a boon. I had previously felt that just getting here was a great achievement, but the old pilgrim was telling me I was destined to change in many other ways.

9

LONDON CALLING

It was cold and dreary on Jaimie's fifth birthday, an early December temperature of sixteen degrees that produced neither joy nor despair. The Lagos squatters' campsite was doing its best to provide Portuguese hospitality, and we did our best to fire up the day for our daughter. We saw *Chicken Little* at the movies, ate McDonald's and ended the day wearing fairy crowns and blowing whistles around a cake in the van. But it was a day indoors, and this promised winter of inclemency had us researching other places to settle. Consequently when Chrissie's text arrived, calling us to London for a flying Christmas visit, we launched off like we'd been offered free seats on the first flight to Mars.

The flights were from Madrid, over a thousand kilometres away, but as they were cheap and saved us a load of money, the week-long backtracking across the plains of Spain was unanimously approved. By the time we arrived there, however, the temperature had dropped to zero and we still had two days in the camper before our UK flights.

Seeking warm indoor entertainment again, we headed for Madrid's Museo del Prado which was reputed as having one of the world's best art collections, many, I told the children, by the ninja turtles Donatello, Raphael, Michelangelo and Leonardo. This would possibly have been quite humorous had they known who the ninja turtles were. But this visit promised to be one of our finest cultural experiences and would entertain the kids because they loved seeing all the paintings and statues with bums exposed.

The very first room we entered was filled with colourful paintings. Callum and I had whizzed through the security entrance ahead of the others, so stood waiting. 'Daddy? What's that doggy doing?' he pointed.

Covering the entire wall was a colourful painting of a huge wolf-like creature crunching a baby's head in its jaws. The baby had a justifiably surprised look on its face. Blood cascaded out of the wolf's mouth and down its neck. The severed carcass of the baby lay at the animal's feet, spurting blood in an arch out of its exposed neck.

Realising that Goya's baby-eating period would be difficult to explain to a two-year-old, I quickly spun him into the next room to face another wall of colour. 'Look over here.'

He stood holding my hand in silence as we absorbed the new scene. It depicted a writhing mass of chunky naked men and women with their genitalia intertwined, participating with vigour in a rather rambunctious, drunken medieval orgy.

Jaimie came running over and gave it her art review. 'Callum… look!' she giggled. 'Bums!'

The limited PG-rated viewing meant we exited the Prado sooner than desired.

Our accommodation in the UK was to doss on the floor with Chrissie at her friend Clair's house, a beautiful old Victorian home in South London. Our hosts were embarrassed about being unable to offer us beds, not realising that our anticipation of waking up without slamming our heads into a ceiling would be luxury.

This season Clair was hosting a squadron of relatives as well as us Australian blow-ins. When we arrived, activity was ramping up as though they were preparing for the D-Day landing.

'I'm late, I'm late! We've got a lot to prepare!' Clair scurried past us like Alice's rabbit. She was attempting to be the hostess with the mostess, trying to ensure all her relatives' disparate Christmas traditions were going to be met. She'd had phone calls for two days with a series of requests specifying favoured bonbon colours and such.

'Pete!' she yelled to her boyfriend. 'Where the fuck is Aunty Sue's dessert spoon? She'll die if it's not on the table.'

Pete rolled his eyes and wandered off to tear apart a cupboard. We tried to stay invisible and pretend not to hear Clair's screams from the hallway: 'I forgot the fucking custard!'

That was my cue. I rallied our clan and we disappeared to get the custard, throwing ourselves into the human Monopoly board that is central London. We rode the dodgem cars in Leicester Square, counted the bongs on Big Ben and watched street theatre in Covent Garden. It was bitingly cold, so like Madrid, indoor museums and cafés became our preferred venues. But in our holiday revelry, two phone calls were about to land like scud missiles that would change the path of our travels forever.

It was early morning on 22 December when Mandy was called to the phone. She came back and rustled me awake. 'Mum and Dad are coming!'

My in-laws, Esther and Rodney, were the ultimate grey nomads, having been travelling Australia in a caravan for the past decade. 'Where? Why?' I rubbed my eyes. 'For Christmas? Clair's not going to like that.'

'No! They've just bought a camper on the internet. They're coming to join us in Europe in six weeks' time.'

It took me a while to absorb this. Mandy's parents were in their late sixties and Rodney's health had been pretty poor for the past few years. They'd been forced to limit their wanderings and stay close to hospitals. I knew Esther had always wanted to travel overseas but it seemed her chance had gone. The idea of them coming over was bordering on outrageous and I liked it immediately. I even got a little kick out of the thought that we may have inspired them in a small way. Until the sombre reality hit me. 'Hang on. They're joining us?'

The dynamics of our 'four of us' family time would alter with others around. I'd only just transcended to this new level of family attentiveness and needed to cement it in place. I wanted to see them. That would be fun. But I didn't want to travel with anyone for any period of time.

Mandy quickly slapped me out of this negativity. 'Come on. It'll be great! Enjoy Christmas… worry about that later.'

The next day, Christmas conviviality was overtaken by Clair's planned military operation. I thought I'd inject some Australian flavour into the proceedings. 'I'll go and get some stubbies.'

The room went silent. 'What are stubbies?'

'Little bottles of beer.'

The room stayed silent. 'Oh... good,' came the doubting reply. 'We never have beer at Christmas. That should be... different.'

I sensed that 'different' was not part of Clair's overall master plan.

'Is there anything else we can help with?' I changed the topic.

Pete pounced, asking if we wanted to do the potatoes.

Mandy quickly agreed, latching on to what she considered the easiest of jobs, given her family would traditionally eat their way through a field of potatoes at Christmas.

'Excellent, but you have to use this.' Pete handed over a smelly plastic bucket.

I read the label. 'What do we do with duck fat?'

He looked at me as though I needed special care. 'You rub it on the spuds, of course.'

'Duck fat. Oh yeah, the only way! It's tradition!' Clair called out, confirming it had been given executive approval.

I glanced at Mandy over Pete's shoulder, hoping she was a duck fat aficionado, but she was busy pretending to stick a finger down her throat.

It was the morning of Christmas Eve when I was dragged out of bed to take the second game-changing phone call. I scribbled notes, listened and went upstairs to rustle Mandy awake. 'Max just called.' He was a good mate of mine in Australia. 'He wants to know if we want a job.'

Mandy rubbed her eyes. 'Why are you swearing at me with that three-letter j word?'

I explained his proposal. He wanted to buy a travel business and needed someone to do the groundwork for him in London. It was exactly what I did in my recent previous life. Mandy had also previously helped set up Flight Centre in the UK, so she knew all the local licensing issues. It would be a six-week project, providing us with accommodation and expenses.

We looked at each other in amazement. It was as though he had been reading our minds because we had been dreading holing up somewhere over winter in southern Europe's dreary non-weather. The timing of the project aligned perfectly with Rod and Esther's arrival and would also stem the flow of our depleting cash reserves, which in turn opened up the opportunity for us to travel beyond twelve months. I could think of no better Christmas present.

We jumped around and celebrated until the sombre reality hit me. 'But it does mean we would have to work!' That stopped the dancing. 'It's not an offer to have a free holiday, you know. Unfortunately people don't pay money for that.'

We sat pondering for a while. The biggest project my mind had worked on in the past six months was a mouse hunt and that had proven somewhat dubious in its effectiveness. My work brain was a flat battery and I liked that. I looked down at my hiking boots. 'I don't even have a pair of shoes to wear to a meeting.'

The kids were giggling at our feet and playing with toy cars. The silent conversation was that neither of us really wanted to snap out of the travel zone. Getting back on the road in our rolling box promised too much fun. But the relief of not spending money would also be fantastic. I felt I was in a game show and Max was the host. 'Choose now,' he was yelling, 'the money or the box!'

My brain hurt. It was too hard, so we made the only decision we could. We decided not to decide.

There were twenty-two people crammed around the long Christmas table on the big day. It was snowing outside, something I had adamantly assured the kids would not happen in London, and as such my promises were further discredited. A fire was raging in the corner, Bing Crosby was singing 'White Christmas' and everyone was drinking my cold beers and commenting on how 'different' it was to have beer at Christmas. The military operation had delivered an unrivalled feast of golden turkey, glazed ham and a mountain of accoutrements. It was a meal that nomadic campers could only dream of.

Everyone liked our duck-fat glazed spuds, but I complained to Chrissie how disgusting and hard it had been to rub the cold goo all over the potatoes.

'You were supposed to heat the fat up first, you plonker,' she advised, 'not stick your hands in it.'

As my glass of beer slipped out of my hand for the third time, I could see that would have been a better strategy.

Chris and I then went outside into the snow and discussed Max's offer. She subtly played the temptress, hinting at all the things we could do together in London, but held back from overtly trying to influence me. After all, she was the one who continued to forego money for her dream of writing. At a party once, a successful lawyer friend of hers had said, 'I don't know how you can live on so little money.' To which she had replied, 'I can't understand how people sell their time so cheaply to do the things they hate.'

I slipped back into the party just in time to witness Callum whack his head into a wall. He mounted a scream worthy of an opera soprano, as I crouched down and opened my arms to him. He ran up, past Mandy, eyes bulging, stopped and then launched into me. 'Daaaaa-deee!' I held him long and tight as his sobs subsided and heard someone say, 'Gee, I would have thought he'd run to his mother for that.' Excluding his bruised head, this was the greatest Christmas present of all.

Mandy would later tell me how bittersweet this moment was for her, happy for me, but feeling the pang of knowing she was no longer the solo sun the kids' world revolved around.

I talked with Max again on Boxing Day and told him my reservations. 'My brain is slow and I have no shoes.' He said he already knew the first and Vinnies could fix the second.

My visions of a flat with internal heating, a six-week spending hiatus and a fridge full of Marks and Spencer lamb shanks also killed off any obstacles to accepting his offer. Mandy could even get another haircut.

'It's the real world compromise, isn't it?' I said to Mandy. 'You have to earn money to do what you want. So you compromise and do stuff you don't want to. And then you end up having so little time left after doing the stuff you didn't want to do that you don't do what you wanted to do in the first place!'

She nodded at my tautological outburst.

But the offer, the place, the people and the time all seemed to align with so many benefits that it was simply too good a gift horse to ignore. I grabbed the proverbial microphone and screamed to the presenter. 'We'll take the money!' (and the shoes and the heating). 'The box can sit in Madrid.'

But the studio audience in my head weren't clapping. I should have noticed the danger sign.

We soon moved to our new home for the month of January, a one-bedroom ex-council flat just off Wimbledon Broadway. We charged in, as had become our ritual when entering an abode without wheels, and ran around fawning over the modern conveniences at our disposal. Central heating, a TV, a bathtub, a washing machine, flush toilets! The kids jumped up and down on the bed – an activity that would have given them concussion in Franki. We both stood in awe looking at the dishwasher as though it were a rare antiquity. Buckingham Palace has over 600 rooms. Our 45-square-metre abode, slightly larger than a generous hotel room, had three. To us, anything that had more than a two-ring burner for a kitchen was a palace.

We settled in quickly and filled the fridge with Marks and Spencer pre-cooked meals. Within a week we were talking with business brokers, scampering around greater London viewing businesses and researching transfer laws. I bought a jacket and black shoes from the local charity shop. Had I stopped to think, I would have noticed how quickly and merrily I was back riding the corporate horse.

This work activity swirled around the children who had been in bliss with all the Christmas attention and presents and snow. But after we moved into the apartment the reality of our new circumstance set in. The two worlds of work and home life fell into an old familiar routine of juggling and sharing. Mandy and I took turns to entertain the kids while the other was working.

It was so bitterly cold that we could do very little outside. I took the kids to the Polka Theatre one day to watch a teddy bear show. Mandy took them to a bookshop with a kids' play area on another. The local shopping centre had a kids' club, so we dropped them there a few times so we could discuss the project together. At night we were so shagged that we fell into a trance watching *Celebrity Big Brother* before passing out. We stopped talking at night. We stopped having family dinners together, instead sitting beside each other at the screen. After long periods of enforced sexual abstinence in the camper, the separate bedroom meant we should have been at it like rabbits, but we were too wasted for even that.

One morning in the third week, I was poring over papers spread out over the tiny lounge room floor. Mandy was writing emails and making calls. The kids rushed out in their pyjamas and jumped happily into my papers.

'What are you doing?' I yelled. 'I told you to stay in the bedroom while we were working!'

Mandy shushed us all angrily, waving with her hand as she was on the phone.

Both the kids burst into tears. 'Why are you working? This is our Franki holiday!' Jaimie ran out, crying.

I followed them back into the bedroom and tried explaining what we were doing.

'But it's our holiday,' she repeated.

Exasperated, I set up the TV in the bedroom and soon they sat happily entranced by the digital babysitter. Problem solved. I had managed to get them out of my way. Just like I used to do.

But I was not completely ignorant. The kids were crying out for the attention they'd become accustomed to and we had reverted to giving them time scraps. It was Friday, so I suggested we take the weekend off and have some dedicated family time.

Mandy almost collapsed in relief at the idea. 'I feel so guilty,' she said. 'All we've done is fallen back into even worse habits than last year. I've spent no real quality time with the kids.'

I rationalised that for the past six months we'd had unsustainable family time, but that too was her point. Why was it unsustainable? Why had I overnight stopped looking at things with new eyes?

Max arrived in London soon after and he and I spent the next weekend with a venture capitalist in Cornwall. We stayed in a beautiful historic pub that sat on one of the old stagecoach routes. It had low timber raked ceilings and wood shavings on the floor and we supped on roast duck and thick soup with croutons. The accompanying potatoes had been done in duck fat, of course. I'd forgotten what it was like to have an expense account. I'd forgotten how much I liked having disposable cash.

In our conversations Max floated the idea that there could be an ongoing role for me in London. I laughed at the notion, but I was interested. And he knew it.

As the business hunt continued, Mandy filled her spare time catching up with Chris. Each day I walked the 500 metres home from Wimbledon train station to our flat. After having spent months in the camper with no real exposure to newspapers or TV, and with no disposable cash, I was intensely aware of the tsunami of advertising swamping me. Stumbling down the high street was like floating through some psychedelic drug scene. Windows and signs brightly flashed urgent never-to-be-repeated discounts for every possible thing that went bling or ting. Products promising health, wealth and enjoyment spewed out from every media orifice. Alluring smells pumped out from KFC and Indian curry outlets. In the after-Christmas rush, people were swarming around filling bags with the latest must-haves. I was determined not to get sucked back into this sick gorging madness. Each day I put my head down and ploughed through the sea of mass consumerism.

On one rainy afternoon I burst through the door into the warm sanctuary of the apartment. The kids were being entertained by the digital babysitter. 'What's that?' Mandy looked up from a report she was finishing.

I grasped new boots and iPod speakers to my chest. 'Nothing,' I replied and landed a box of KFC on the table. It was impossible for me to repeatedly pass Colonel Sanders without taking action.

We had only been back in the real world for a short time and already we had been drawn back into obsessive TV watching, overeating, buying crap and tossing the kids time bones. Our lofty goals of changing our lifestyle and seeing things through new eyes when we eventually returned home suddenly seemed like an unrealistic fantasy.

I later looked up from my *News of the World* article about a guy who decided to interbreed with ferrets. 'It can't be done in the real world,' I said forlornly to Mandy.

'What? Bonk ferrets. I hope not!'

'No. That would be easy. Just use masking tape. What can't be done is how we create the simpler, slower life in the real world. We're too weak. We're too conditioned. There's too much temptation.' I was really talking about myself but it sounded better to make it the royal 'we' and include Mandy in my personal downfall.

But there was no one else to blame. It seemed I had reverted to type and sold my soul to the corporate god at the very first chance. I felt like a substance abuser who'd been in the protective rehab of Franki, but as soon as I was out, I was snorting the corporate coke again, drunk for the money, work, ego and assets. On Monday I resumed my duties, feeling conflicted by the fact that I was really enjoying the task. The next week we pulled off a miracle and negotiated a purchase. This to me was a thrill. I loved a successful negotiation. The mind reading. The tactics. The winning result for all. I was back, flexing my muscles in a sport I enjoyed.

By the end of another frenzied working week, we decided to focus on the kids again with a trip to London's Natural History Museum. The dinosaur display area was muted dark and filled with replicas of prehistoric beasts and recreated skeletons. As we approached the end of the chamber, we entered an even darker room to confront a giant robotic Tyrannosaurus Rex with its teeth bared and head swaying. Callum was four paces ahead of us. The T-Rex turned its head and roared out at the line of children. Callum screamed and turned, running towards me. I went down on my haunches and held out my arms to offer a safe sanctuary. He squealed louder at my face, tears pouring down his, and pushed me away.

'Mummy!' he screamed. 'Not you! I want Mummy!' As the giant critter roared again, he rushed past me into Mandy's arms.

Other adults looked at me as I stood back up, embarrassed and hurt by his snub. I brushed myself off and pretended not to care, outwardly smiling at the scene of him huddled into Mandy's bosom. But there it was for all to see. All the gains I'd made over the past six months in becoming a true, compassionate joint parent were being wiped out astonishingly fast by my renewed work commitment. In a few short weeks, the children had become mummy-centric again. It was ironic that I had come to London to connect with friends and now discovered that what I had mostly achieved was a gross disconnect with the children. I had become the absent working father again. I was destroying the one thing that had been my greatest achievement on this journey so far.

Our job in London was virtually completed. I felt relieved as I needed to get away from the tree of temptation. Then Max called again, asking if I would be interested in coming back in a month for good.

An international posting covering Europe, in a role I enjoyed, was a dream opportunity. But the offer also came with one caveat. We would have to stay in touch and give a commitment to return on a month's notice.

'So even if you were just considering it, we'd have to check emails and phones?' Mandy asked.

I nodded, understanding her point. To make any sort of agreement with Max, casual or otherwise, would disembowel our ability to wallow in the travel zone, disconnected from the world with no set times, no end date, nowhere to go, on no one else's agenda. It would kill the life of Franki. Our mindless, endless freedom would be gone. And you don't get many chances at that in your life.

The kids were oddly quiet during the day and must have picked up on our conversations. They both joined forces and came to us sheepishly. They seemed nervous and, as usual, Jaimie was the spokesperson. 'When are we... when are we going home, Mummy?' They focused on her, instinctively knowing she was their best chance of success. She wasn't the corporate addict.

This time there was no misinterpretation. The only place they considered home was Franki. They had no interest in piling up money. They just wanted to be together with us again.

I sat and stared at them for a long time. I thought of Callum running past me in the dinosaur pit and figured this was my one chance to change my life for good. If I turned away now and re-entered work, then I would have failed in my quest for a better way to live. I clearly had not beaten the intoxicating corporate drugs and I had to start taking note of the subtle messages my sage wife and attentive children were sending me.

I cuddled the kids as a silent thank you and felt an overwhelming urge to get back to the safety of the camper where temptation couldn't lure me at every corner. I suddenly couldn't wait to hit my head on the roof when getting out of bed. Or get back to cooking chicken in a pot. Sharing timed, cold showers with the kids. Or wondering where we were going to be on any given day. This freedom and family time was a rare gift we had given ourselves.

The next day, I rang Max, apologised and said we were on our own mission. Maybe one day I'd be ready to talk again. But not now.

I packed my new boots and iPod speakers and closed the door on our apartment for good. We headed back out on the road. I was more resolved to make lasting changes to how I lived my life, but far less certain that I had it in me to ever make it possible.

10

THE QUEST FOR EVERYTHING

I had always thought of monkeys as cute fluffy little things, a type of koala. But the ones that patrolled the summit of the Rock of Gibraltar were not cute at all. These guys had bloodshot eyes, long fangs and wandered around as though they were between rounds in a fight club.

'Look at the monkeys!' Callum pointed.

I dragged my eyes away from the glistening blue water stretching along the rugged Spanish coastline. 'They're actually Barbary macaques, matey.'

Callum frowned. He was going through a stage in which he would adamantly correct any grammar that didn't align with his reality. 'Not Barbie marks... monkeys!' he yelled.

I held up my hands, having learnt not to argue with this potential scream bubble when he entered his pernickety mode. 'OK... monkeys then. Just chill out, man.' I turned away and whispered 'Barbary macaques' to myself in some form of personal linguistic victory over my infant son.

'I think he's hungry,' Mandy suggested. 'Can you get his Vegemite sandwich out of my daypack?'

Mandy turned with the pack still on her back. I ferreted away, rustling noisily through various plastic bags.

'Dad-deee!' Callum cried out.

'Shush, mate! I'm getting it. Wait!' Digging through my wife's assorted bags was like reaching into the junk section of a kleptomaniac's purse. 'If you hadn't packed so much sh—'

I heard a hiss and looked up to see a tooth-baring ape soaring through the air towards us. Instantly, I reacted to this danger to my wife with the instincts of a special agent protecting the president. I lurched out of the way, squealing.

The ape landed on Mandy's back. She launched into a frenzied screaming spin. It was then I saw the large red-lettered sign on the fence: *Beware! Apes associate plastic bags with food and will snatch.*

The macaque clung on, grabbing Mandy's hair with one hand like he was riding a rodeo bull and tearing inside the pack with the other. As Mandy, the human spinning top, increased her velocity, I tried valiantly not to laugh. The ape eventually ripped the plastic bag out and vaulted over the fence. Mandy threw the daypack off like it was a strap-on bomb and hurtled into the nearby café. The macaque sat down on a stony outcrop and slowly, tauntingly, picked his way through the prize.

Callum was apoplectically distraught, having never seen his mother attacked by a wild animal before. 'Daddy! Daad-deee!' Tears sprayed from his eyes.

'It's OK, Callum.' I knelt and cuddled him, still trying to harness my inappropriate convulsions of laughter. 'Mummy's safe now.'

'But Daaaa-deeee!' he screamed louder than ever. 'A monkey took my sandwich!'

Fortunately no one had noticed my cowardly retreat, including Rod and Esther. As the story was repeated, Rodney's grin kept spreading. 'Lucky we came here.'

'Why's that?'

'Well, Mandy's always wanted to come to Gibraltar,' he said deadpan. 'Now she's finally got that monkey off her back.'

He and I thought that was the funniest thing we had ever heard and fell apart laughing.

We'd been doing a lot of laughing since Rod and Esther had joined us in Madrid a fortnight earlier. Although I was excited to see them, I was still harbouring concerns about group travel. Particularly now that I was keen to hit the road aimlessly again and wash my London downfall away. I knew from previous group adventures that even small issues like agreeing on what time to depart in the morning could lead to long debates and unwanted compromise.

Esther was a practical woman. I knew she'd have researched a few must-sees and we'd have to allow for them, but I certainly didn't want to get caught chasing a sightseeing list and trying to do everything and go everywhere.

'So what's your plan, guys?' I asked them a day after their arrival.

'Well,' she announced, throwing her arms wide. 'I want to do everything. I want to go everywhere!'

With that narrow goal clarified and ringing in my head, she charged to her van and re-emerged with a long sightseeing list. I stared at the book in horror. It had taken me years to brainwash planning out of my wife and now her mother had turned up with a list of lists.

Since then we'd commenced working through Esther's Spain list.

We'd been to Segovia to see its 700-metre-long granite aqueduct with over 150 arches. It was the greatest aqueduct I had ever seen, making my aqueduct strike rate one for one.

The hill town of Ávila had a preserved city wall walk second only to Dubrovnik.

Toledo, the former capital of the Spanish empire, had impressive fortified walls that enclosed the city and a towering Gothic cathedral within.

And after we'd visited the Alhambra, Granada's hilltop ancient palace cum royal residence, fortress and mini-city that was one of the modern wonders of the world, I had to admit I was starting to enjoy having a well-prepared tour guide on board.

'Well that's one thing off the list,' Esther declared as we left Gibraltar. 'But I'm going to need more than one lifetime to do it all.'

With her list, I thought, she was going to need ten.

When I shared this thought, she replied, 'Well it's all right for you guys. You have years ahead of you. This may be our one and only chance!'

This reply pulled me up. They were living proof of the 'never too old' adage. Our fresh-faced travelling companions were like puppies off a leash and I couldn't help but get caught up in their infectious excitement. They possessed an almost childish awe of everything we were doing. Every coffee, glass of frosty San Miguel and tasty tapas became a new collegiate adventure for us all. I watched them playing with the kids or chatting with locals and realised how they were drinking in this experience of travel because they thought their chance had passed.

When Rodney later told me they couldn't get travel insurance to cover his heart, I thought that was a gutsy call, given he'd had a number of attacks. When I suggested to Esther that it was a bit like playing Russian roulette, she replied, 'Yeah we know that,' and then detailed how in the past few years they'd hardly left Brisbane, feeling like all they'd been doing was visiting doctors. 'It was as though we were just waiting, but for nothing. And then, when we told people we intended buying a camper in Europe, they all told us we were mad.'

I laughed. 'Dream stealers.'

'Exactly. Everyone said we were too old. Too sick. That we were spending our kids' inheritance. But the idea of doing this...' She waved her arms around.

'You mean everything?'

'Yes, John... everything. The idea gave us so much happiness. We felt like we were living again. We decided that if we were going to die on this trip, at least we'd be doing something we loved.'

I nodded thoughtfully. 'Are you sure about spending the kids' inheritance?'

After Mandy got that monkey off her back in Gibraltar, we began plotting our time together.

'Morocco!' Esther declared. 'I've always wanted to go there.'

She really did want to take this 'do everything' quest to another level.

'Morocco! Africa,' she repeated at our surprised faces.

'Yeah, I know, but will it be safe for the kids?' There had recently been violent protests outside Western embassies across many Muslim countries and one of the first things the two grandparents wanted to do was take our family troupe traipsing around Muslim North Africa. It was ludicrous.

But Mandy and I smiled at each other. The zing-zing of a 'walk the plank and jump' adventure was back. Maybe this group travel thing wasn't going to be too bad after all.

I soon announced a shortcut to Tangier, which excited Rodney until Mandy suggested that following my shortcuts was akin to a baby lamb springing into a mincing machine.

I ignored her, insisting we could go via a high speed catamaran from the small Spanish town of Tarifa, which would be quicker and 200 euros cheaper than going from Algeciras, one of Spain's largest ports.

'Catamaran?' Mandy pounced. 'Wouldn't that be rougher than a normal ferry?' She had become paranoid about sea crossings since her Lofotens vomitathon.

I scanned the brochure's fine print. *The catamarans, while much quicker, are significantly more prone to rough weather than the ferry.* Then I confirmed the price again – a

200-euro saving. I looked up at her. 'Nah. No worries. She'll be right.'

With that declaration, I might as well have rung God Himself and ordered a storm for the day of our crossing. As our craft bunny-hopped through the huge seas heaving in from the Atlantic and up the Strait of Gibraltar, Mandy disappeared to hurl her lungs out. I felt terribly guilty, and knew exactly what I must do.

I tore up the brochure with the incriminating fine print.

When we arrived at Tangier customs we were still concerned about the reception we Westerners might get. This was heightened when a soldier with a string of bullets draped over his shoulder wiggled his finger at Rodney and me and said, 'Come.'

Our first thoughts went to the stash of wine we had on board our campers. Idiots! Muslim country! Alcohol. Illegal. Hands cut off. The second, the logical fear of anyone pulled aside into a customs room, was anal probing. This was Rodney's first border crossing involving heavily armed militia and I could see he was gravitating towards panic. Fortunately, I was experienced in these situations and was able to calm him. 'We're fucked,' I whispered.

Inside the customs room, more guards were leaning on their guns, smoking and playing cards. A picture of King Mohammed VI was on the wall. 'Don't joke about the king,' I whispered; another gem of wisdom for Rodney, as though he was always making king jokes.

The guard then broke into a huge grin that made him look more like a naughty boy than a coup leader and explained we had to register our vehicles.

Once done, all was good and the only probing was my one question. 'How much time will it take to get to Rabat?'

'Aaah, Rabat!' The big man rocked back in his undersized squeaky chair and scratched his chin slowly. 'I am thinking… about as long as it takes you… to drive your vehicles there.'

We stood, exchanging glances, absorbing this infallible logic. And then I smiled. We were on African time now.

Separating us from Tangier proper was a chain wire fence with an army of children clinging to it and a crowd of shouting hawkers behind them. Leaving everything child-safe, orderly and European behind us, I now knew how a bull about to be released into the Coliseum felt.

Outside, old black Mercedes taxis wheeled around with music and horns blasting. Battered tip-trucks overflowed with people. Hot dusty fumes poured through our windows, bringing a psychotic aroma of fried spices and old motel carpet. There were no decipherable road rules or signs. Traffic police waved their arms around like drowning swimmers, directing a maelstrom of people clad in white robes, fez hats and black burqas. None were toting guns, or screaming 'Die, infidel!' as the media would have us expect, but our bourgeois machines still felt like a glowing target of Western affluence.

We weaved along as I barked instructions like a confused army general under heavy fire. 'Just keep going,' I cried. 'Eventually I'll know where we are.'

Somehow we miraculously found our way to the southern highway, and stopped on the roadside to regroup.

'Bloody hell! That was extreme,' I said to Mandy. 'Great driving!'

She looked at me as though I'd just proposed marriage. 'You've never complimented my driving before.'

We looked into each other's eyes, but our loving bubble was quickly burst by Rodney blasting his horn from behind. They had been following us so close it appeared as though we were towing them. He was warning us of an approaching swarm of children who now jumped up and pulled at my arm calling 'Mister! Mister! You give money!'

'Let's go!' I cried.

After the romp through Tangier's battle zone, we chose Salé's Camping la Plage because the guidebook stated it was secure. We arrived to find it was enclosed by a high mud brown wall topped with razor wire and broken glass. Exposed electrical wires draped through water puddles.

'It's secure,' Mandy observed dryly.

I decided to take the kids to shower and freshen up, opening the first shower cubicle to face a pile of human excrement. We scurried back outside, gasping for air, and I instantly promoted Franki's toilet/shower to the number one accessory for Morocco.

We all fell asleep, exhausted, but were promptly woken in the dawn's early light.

'Waaaaaaaah, waaaaaaaaahhh!' A symphony of dying cats was bleating out across the land.

I lurched up, slamming my head into the roof, before slowly recognising the Islamic call to prayer that was going to assault us five times a day from dawn for the next month.

Dodgy power. Shit-filled showers. Chaotic roads. Dawn wailing and rioters behind every lamp post. I was really beginning to wonder about this 'do everything' quest that had led us here.

That day, we explored Salé's medina, a still fully intact walled enclosure that was a throwback to medieval days. We plunged through the nearest city gate into a maze of narrow laneways. In Western dress, we may as well have been glowing and very soon, a mob crowded in, touching and pulling at us. Jaimie and Callum were buffeted around and it was some minutes before I realised that it was the kids' blue eyes and Jaimie's blonde hair that was the attraction. We kept moving through laneways of spices, clothes, engine parts and animals, patting chameleons and dodging blood dripping from the decapitated heads of various livestock. A growing retinue of women and children followed, chortling at our every expression and lining up to kiss the kids' foreheads.

Mandy soon relaxed and was drawn to a barber's stripy pole and mimed an unusual mixture of snipping actions so he would cut Callum's hair.

'Does he understand you?' I asked.

'Yes, of course. My miming is great. It's obvious, a trim.'

Soon a congregation crowded around to watch the little foreign boy get his hair cut. I wandered off and returned when the mob was applauding. Callum had a bowl of hair on the top of his head and was shaved bald down from just above his ears. He looked like a cross between a Buddhist monk and Mo from The Three Stooges.

He was beaming with pride, accepting false plaudits of how cute he looked. Jaimie noticed the attention he was getting and asked, 'Can I get my hair cut too?'

'No!' Esther and I cried in unison.

After this rock star welcome, we lost our trepidation, reaffirming what the sensationalist press fails to do: that Muslims were more likely to toss us gifts than bombs.

Days later we were huddled inside Casablanca's Camping Oasis, after driving through a landscape that had looked like a flaming meteor shower had just hit. Potholes were the size of cars. Fires burnt in bins with animals roasting on grills and sending smoke skywards. Our big machines had swayed through the traffic that swirled as though people were evacuating in both directions, all road markings arbitrarily ignored by donkeys, carts and overloaded buses.

A local woman was cooking a chicken tajine for us, braised over a fire and loaded with olives, prunes, fruit and spices. She had already laid white tablecloths over our camp tables and set places with silver cutlery.

While waiting, the kids ran around and Rodney loaded us up with head-slamming gin and tonics, his own signature dish of the past weeks. I suspected they were also designed to deaden us from the heightened challenges of this vast country. I wondered how long the grandparents, more accustomed to Western niceties and traffic that respected road lines, would be able to cope.

Esther soon answered that question. 'I wish we'd done this years ago!' she exclaimed.

'What? Drank G and T triples?' Mandy laughed.

'Yeah, that too. No, everything. This!' she waved her hands at the star-filled sky.

'At least you're doing it now,' I said. 'Even after everyone kept telling you it was too late.'

'Yes, but it sort of is. You know, people always think that when you're young, you can work and save and you will have plenty of time later to do the things you wish for. And then time is gone, flashed past in a blink.'

I simmered on this comment. I was forty-two and had heaps of time, but forty-two was Esther's yesterday. It would be my yesterday just as quick and time would be up. Do I live for the now like a drunken sailor in port or be responsible and plan for the future? My own quest for everything was getting blurry.

The dark alleys of the souk markets of the former imperial city of Marrakech ran through its ancient medina. They were filled with jewellery, clothes, beautiful timber furniture, coloured carpets, brass, copper, polished silver, bright wool and newborn animals. Everything glittered and sparkled as though we were inside Aladdin's cave. These markets had been the main trading hub in North Africa for a thousand years. They radiated old-fashioned, raw tradition. Nothing had changed, there were no signs of Western influence anywhere.

'Mister!' one trader cried. 'We take American Express!'

Once it was discovered we were Australian, Bondi Beach, Mad Max and AC/DC became the main topics of conversation in the souk, closely followed by how splendiferous my golden-haired daughter looked, and how wise, fatherly, excellent and blessed with good fortune I was. Resisting the charm-offensive, I refused to be lured into their buying traps, particularly when one chap, with a small ape on his shoulder, overplayed his hand and insisted I needed a set of timber doors.

'Thanks,' I smiled. 'We have a camper. No room.'

'Aah! Camper. Good. I find something perfect.'

He came back with a bird in a wooden cage.

Jaimie and I later rejoined the others in the massive, dusty Djemaa el-Fna, the medina's main square. Mandy had purchased one item, while I looked like I'd been shopping with Paris Hilton at a Vegas discount outlet.

The sun soon went down in a blaze of orange as the *adhan* wailed out, sparking an echo of wails from other minarets across the city. Its message that there was no God except the one God began. This melodic wail, initially annoying, now joyfully transported me to another world.

The Djemaa el-Fna during the day was a spectacle of Moroccan life, but as the moon rose in the blue desert sky, the square started flooding with people. Tents were erected. Fires created multiple plumes of smoke. Colourful troupes entertained. Monkeys leapt around. Old soothsayers sat cross-legged under black umbrellas. Storytellers were surrounded by men who erupted into sporadic laughter, cheers and 'ooohs'. 'Dentists' were selling hundreds of teeth, their source of supply curiously undeclared.

Marrakech's medina had been the inaugural inclusion in UNESCO's Masterpieces of the Oral and Intangible Heritage of Humanity. We decided to be part of this human masterpiece.

As we jostled our way around, I was mindful of the kids' safety and the invariable attention their presence attracted. At one display, I stopped to admire colourful spices, but when I turned around, my family had disappeared into the robed masses. I heard Callum's distinctive squeal and instantly pictured him being stashed in the back of a cart and sold off to some sheik. I pushed my way towards the scream to find Jaimie sitting in the middle of a cleared circle. A small fire was in front of her. Adjacent, a man sat cross-legged playing a flute.

I slowly absorbed the scene, recoiling in horror as though I'd just walked into Norman Bates' bathroom.

A black cobra was upright, swaying its head back and forth inches from Jaimie's face. Two more snakes were draped over her, two she held in her hands. She was grinning like a hyena.

I sidled across to Mandy, forcing words out as though I had a car part in my throat. 'What the fuck… are you doing?'

'Shsssh!' she slapped my arm. 'Get a photo. And one of Dad too.'

Rodney had a pathological dislike for snakes that was second only to my own. I looked past Mandy to see him sitting on the ground with a blue *Lawrence of Arabia* keffiyeh scarf wrapped around his head. He was kissing a cobra on the lips.

Going in and out of Marrakech's medina over the following days was like having a pass to an amusement park. In between jaunts, we pottered around writing letters, filling water tanks and sweeping sand out of the vans.

The kids were having fun just playing in the dirt, until one afternoon Callum let out a long, high-pitched squeal, his fourth in succession.

In response I stormed out of the camper. 'Callum! I. Have. Told. You. To stop… that! Screaming is totally unacceptable!' I screamed.

I was interrupted by the arrival of two giant blue and gold peacocks. They scampered across the dirt and stood over Callum, fanning out their massive wings to a colourful six-foot span, bobbing their heads, raking their feet and screeching at him.

I didn't know whether his squeal was interpreted by the peacocks as a war cry or a mating request, but figured it was best not to visualise either result. Callum froze. The peacocks kept flapping and stomping until he sprang up, dived into the camper and yanked his bed curtains closed.

The birds slowly deflated and strolled off.

'It must have been terrifying for the little tyke,' I wrote to my mum that night. 'However, *Peacock screech in a bottle: How to shut a three-year-old up!* would be a bestseller.'

After Marrakech, we began a slow foray south and the windows of Franki became our entertainment screen. Field-working families would see our two white vans rolling across the plains, drop their tools, abandon their goats and ox-drawn ploughs, and run to stand roadside and wave.

South of Agadir, however, the hand waving from field workers was replaced by small kids brandishing plastic bottles of murky liquid at us.

It took some research to discover that the local argan oil in these bottles was resold in fashionable boutiques around the world. These kids' parents had developed a fast oil harvesting method so they could cash in. Rather than wait for the argan nuts to shed their shell by naturally falling to the ground, they got their goats to climb the trees and eat the unripened nuts. The shells dissolved in the goats' stomach and later, the family sifted through the goat shit to retrieve the inner nut, which they then cooked and squeezed the oil out.

Unfortunately, their trade was being impacted on as Western buyers demanded certification that the oil being rubbed on their faces was naturally extracted and not a by-product of goat-shit extraction. The roadside kids weren't scamming us, they were just doing what kids do in the Sahara. Not going to school. Not getting an education. But working from the time they could walk, to help their family survive.

It was the start of a conundrum that would overwhelm us all as we sailed our ships of wealth across Morocco through a sea of poverty.

Within hours of moving east away from the coast at Sidi Ifni on a path towards the Saharan ergs, we entered a remote, inhospitable landscape. With the Atlas Mountains on our left and the Algerian border to the south, it was a land with few people and no cars, just a long expanse of stony nothing.

Many of the desert dwellers out here were Berbers, descendants of the original occupiers of the great kingdoms of North Africa. The ones still living off the land were mostly illiterate and uneducated, descended from noble origins to now be Morocco's lowest caste. Men and women, old before their time, often had sun-drenched dark faces caving in around their mouths from lack of teeth. It was a tough life out here with no wealth, no health support, few clothes and short life expectancies.

We soon found that every venture to buy food, petrol or coffee became a thrill. People would kiss and pat our kids, offering mint tea and food. This shared commonality, of children, parents and grandparents together, tearing the hinges off the doors of hospitality.

The family clusters we stopped roadside to say hello to possessed none of the glazed eyes and insistent begging of the urban downtrodden. Their kids' smiles could light up a nation and the only thing they proactively asked for was pencil and paper. Not money.

Esther and I had bought some plastic footballs and gave them out to the kids as we went. I'll never know if we were helping or hindering them. What would happen when the ball bust or was deflated? Would this ruin their joy at playing with paper balls held together by string? The starburst of joy these offerings evoked convinced me we were doing the right thing, but maybe I was just another well-intentioned Westerner, making myself feel good by intervening, without seeking to understand what the people wanted in the first place.

Our two vans rumbled on. Through Tafraoute, the Amtoudi Oasis, Tata, Zagora, the lush green Draa Valley with a ruined kasbah at every turn. A sign said 'Tombouctou. 52 jours'.

I had travelled through various African countries pre-marriage, pre-kids. Hitching, riding trains and trucks, bartering for boiled eggs and learning to suck sugar cane to survive. It was not something I yearned to repeat with small children. But in the past with only my backpack, I had not felt the chasm between wealth and poverty so acutely as I did now.

Franki was a constant symbol of this divide, worth an unimaginable bounty here and providing extraordinary luxuries like food, roof and bedding.

Having the kids with us made me want to save every other child we met.

Yet travelling with Rodney and Esther also opened my eyes. Each night, we would sip G and T's together, counting satellites among the blistering array of stars, as they joined Mandy and I in our musings. The poverty around us was constantly at the front of our minds and we all agreed the families we had seen made us appreciate our own even more.

The family entity was central to the Islamic way of life. They shared success and shame and revered their older community members. Listening to their elders was considered an opportunity for wisdom and spiritual growth. In travelling with Mandy's parents, our own elders, I had started to relate to this.

I now realised that Esther's quest wasn't about doing everything. It was about her grabbing time with fervour. To hang with these two, who knowingly had fewer days ahead of them than behind, whacked me with a sense of urgency that Mandy and I also had to grab time by the scruff of the neck. Because as Esther had said at Gibraltar, this was our one and only chance.

After many glorious driving days, the township of Merzouga and the dunes of Erg Chebbi came into view. From a distance, the 250-metre-high erg looked like orange pyramids. Its ridgeline was perfect, as though drawn by a pencil. The lifeless grey desert and the cloudless bright blue sky contrasted its impossibly orange bulk, like an exaggerated Michelangelo painting.

We squeezed the vehicles into the rear of a kasbah, angling them up to the point where the erg met the stones, creating a floor of Saharan sand under the awnings. Once parked, the kids shot out of Franki and launched into the world's largest sandpit.

We rode dromedaries into the desert two days later, leaving pre-dawn on four giant beasts that were flamboyantly clad in Berber head gear as though they were going to a camel wedding. As the sun rose and the sands changed through a spectrum of colours, I rode supporting my back and Callum sang through the alphabet, while Rodney swayed along as though he was drunk. Only the girls, with Esther doubling Jaimie, had this camel thing under control. 'We're more used to dealing with smelly annoying animals,' Mandy explained later.

The big erg was challenging us to climb it. 'It'll be a piece of piss!' I convinced Mandy, as we trudged off two days later.

The kids stayed with Rod and Esther and, within a dozen paces, I realised this was a rare moment in the past eight months when Mandy and I were alone together. The family camping lifestyle didn't offer much privacy, so I naturally suggested the one opportunity this twosome time provided. Sex in the Saharan sand. What a boast that would be at parties where everyone competed for the craziest place they'd 'done it'.

Since embarking on our journey, we had become somewhat proficient at silent tantric manoeuvres in the night that didn't rock the van. I even considered putting a sticker on Franki like surfers once did with their vans – *Don't come a' knockin' if this van's a' rockin'*. Or another renowned sticker, adapted for grey nomads: *Don't laugh – it could be your mother inside!*

With the sun beating down, we began our ascent, feet sinking with every step – twenty paces, stop, suck water, and start again. I would pass Mandy, and then she me as I lay panting. 'Peeth of pith,' I gasped, spitting sand out of my mouth.

Halfway up and we were spent, so decided it was an ideal place for a sandy romp. But then Mandy held her hand up and pointed. 'Oh, no. Look!'

A squadron of schoolchildren was running across the sands. 'Ohhh!' I groaned. 'Is there any escaping from kids?'

We were soon run down by a stampede of screaming teens, pushing and shoving each other up the dune. 'Kangaroo!' one chap yelled and began hopping around. 'I hope you make it,' he taunted.

'Little prick,' I whispered. 'Come on, let's show 'em!' We ploughed on, intermittently collapsing on rubbery legs, but now steely determined to reach the top.

Once at the peak, the teens started rolling back down, until suddenly they were gone. We eventually collapsed at the apex, finally alone. My mouth was dry and our sweaty bodies were encrusted with sand. I spat more sand out and spluttered a most romantic offer that surely no woman could knock back. 'I s'pose thex is out of the question?'

The only roll we had that day was to slide back down the dunes.

Erg Chebbi was our turnaround point. We eventually circled back through Fez to Tangier, detouring to the top of the Atlas Mountains, where a cable car delivered us beyond the 3,000-metre mark to throw snowballs at each other. Snow under the blazing hot sun, this type of mad and confusing contrast reflected our time in Morocco.

On our descent the next day, a squad of local kids scampered down the mountain on steep paths between the snaking road bends so they were waiting for us around every turn.

I threw out my last football, watching it bounce towards a dozen delirious arms. But the smallest of them fumbled it over the road's edge and so the group tumbled down after it like a human avalanche.

I watched and wondered when I last appreciated something so basic with so much vigour. Pencils and paper, a roof, health, even our years ahead. I had relapsed in London, but when it came to material possessions, I was no longer on a quest for everything. I may have finally got that monkey off my back.

11

FOREVER YOUNG

We split from Rod and Esther back in Tarifa and headed on a cross-continent jaunt for four weeks. It was the end of April, off season, campsites were often empty and we missed the collegiate bonhomie of afternoon gin and tonic sessions.

Our days had reverted back to a regular routine. Our morning family bed cuddles would progress to breakfast, dish washing, bed making and applauding Mandy each time she emptied the chemical toilet. The days were filled buying supplies, crawling over playgrounds, playing with teddies, having a siesta, eating gelato, driving and washing clothes in a bucket with a toilet plunger. At nights we would edit photos, read, write letters, have unsatisfying showers, play iPod trivia and solve the problems of the world. We did nothing exceptional, and yet as our travel explorations became indistinguishable from just living life, I started to realise how exceptional that was.

But our comfortable routine was about to be broken. As we drove out of Ioannina in northern Greece, we spotted two rain-drenched hitchhikers huddling under a blue plastic sheet beside new backpacks and holding a soggy sign marked

'Thessaloniki', a hopeful 280-kilometre trip on a day when few cars were going that way. I instantly thought back to when Mandy and I had hitchhiked around Alaska. Back then, I had saved my harshest verbal sprays for the big fat motor homes that cruised past while the bourgeois occupants stared straight outward as though we were invisible. I would shake my fists at the bastards in their disappearing Winnebagos.

We cruised past the two hikers in our big fat motor home, staring straight outward as though they were invisible.

We had recently discussed whether we should pick up hikers after passing two goateed candidates who looked like they'd escaped from their jobs in the latrine of a local prison. 'If they'd just dress neatly,' I had bemoaned. But we agreed that we couldn't expose the kids to such risk. After all, the days of Jack Kerouac's travelling nomads were long gone. Nobody picks up hitchhikers anymore. They are all killers and thieves.

Still, I felt as though I had betrayed a travelling brotherhood. 'Stop!' I yelled. 'Pick 'em up!'

To my surprise, Mandy slammed on the brakes, sliding Franki to a stop. 'You're right,' she cried, having telepathically connected with my thoughts. 'Let's do it!'

I climbed through to the back and opened the side door as the hikers ran up the road. 'I hope they meet my criteria,' I called out. I had previously joked about the only possible conditions under which we should consider offering someone a ride. 'Three non-negotiables! One. Obviously backpackers. Two. Look like swimwear models. Three. Female.'

The hikers ran up to the van, blabbering away in Dutch because they had noted our number plates, and ripped off their rain hoods. Mandy laughed and poked her tongue at me. All three of her conditions had been met. Backpackers, swimwear models, and male.

We did the 'Hello, where are you from, where are you going' introductory review to try and establish in seven seconds if they were card-carrying axe murderers. No obvious psychosis was identifiable, so we shuffled Jaimie and Callum over to the window, making room for the lads at the bench seats.

Baptiste and Ulysses were eighteen and twenty-one, hitchhiking for nine months from Holland to India. Ulysses explained this was their first big trip away from home. 'I have 500 euros, but Baptiste has only 300,' he said.

'To get to Turkey?' I asked.

'No. The whole trip. We left Amsterdam twelve days ago and have spent ten euros.'

'Each?' I was instantly in awe of their tightwad wizardry.

'In total,' Ulysses corrected.

I raised my eyebrows towards Mandy. It didn't take an abacus to work out that their funds were abysmally short. The jury was still out on whether they were axe murderers, but they certainly were fantastic dreamers.

He then explained how they slept in fields or barns, knocking on people's doors and asking for food and shelter. 'We don't wash much,' he lamented.

I could now understand the odour of rotting carpet that had pervaded through the van. 'We should have had more than three non-negotiables,' I whispered to Mandy.

'So what do you guys do?' Baptiste asked brightly as though we were strangers at a dinner party.

This enquiry added annoyance to their wafting body odour, as I had become almost oversensitive to this particular question, believing it inaccurately categorised a person's character by what they do to earn money. Teacher – organised. Accountant – boring. Lawyer – arsehole. Well, maybe there was some merit to this categorisation after all. But I was still fighting to reclaim my own identity from the job it had been intricately linked to for so long. It had been glorious to have been free of this social 'what do you do' judging distortion for months. In fact, we'd spent so much time in splendid isolation rediscovering ourselves that we no longer knew what we did. Consequently, I replied with pinpoint accuracy, 'Bit o' this. Bit o' that. Whatever it is, we're doing it.'

They absorbed this reply, nodding seriously as though I were the Dalai Lama and had said something profound.

I knew from experience that good hitchhikers should mimic the driver. If he's chatty, they should chat. If he is silent, they should shut up. Never open a shaken Coke can in the cabin. Don't scoff all the hosts' food. And it is always best to have showered in recent history. These few things could greatly increase the chances of a long sustained ride.

These guys weren't good hitchhikers, in fact as they devoured our bananas and water like rescued castaways, they were promising to be the hikers from hell. To slow down their gorging consumption rate, we told them about the highlights of our recent drive, coast to coast from Spain to Greece. It was a brief four-minute tour. Barcelona and the Rio-style carnival of its main street, La Rambla, and its amazing church, the Sagrada Família; the discovery of the perfect Spanish beach cove at Calella de Palafrugell; walking Italy's five Mediterranean villages of the Cinque Terre; clambering over Pompeii; eating mussels in white wine at share tables in Sorrento's town square; and jumping off rocks into the Bay of Naples opposite Mount Vesuvius.

'But the highlight,' I announced, 'was Easter!'

'Oh no, Daddy! Don't tell them!' Callum cried, which naturally meant I must. And so I explained in gritty detail how Mandy had insisted that the kids be able to eat as much chocolate as they wanted. It was a harshly debated decision which I lost, deferring to the mother of the children, as men must. Callum consumed his Easter bounty as though a conveyor belt was feeding chocolates into his mouth. This went well until we were on a motorway heading towards the Salvador Dalí museum at Figueres and he projectile-vomited all over the inside of the van. Unable to pull over, I launched around Franki with a plastic bag, trying to catch the brown spew jets like a clumsy goalkeeper in a penalty shootout.

Fortunately, the Dalí museum provided enough statues with bums to distract Callum from more vomiting, so while we tried to understand many of the pieces such as 'Eggs on a plate without the plate', and 'Two pieces of bread expressing the sentiment of love', the kids bounced around giggling at genitalia.

During my tale, the Dutch hitchhikers played with Jaimie's Eastern European Barbie doll and bounced teddies across the table to the delightful squeals of the children. They then proceeded to tell us their own story.

'Have you ever heard of the Rainbow group?' Ulysses asked enthusiastically. 'We met lots of people at the Europe Rainbow gathering last year. They have been helping us too, just like this!'

I was starting to wonder what his definition of 'just like this' exactly was, and how it applied to us, particularly as they had now consumed all our fruit.

As we drove east, the snow-capped Pindos mountain range progressively filled our view. In between, when their mouths weren't munching on something out of our fridge, we chatted about Kurt Cobain, world politics and, of course, their travel quest. It was becoming quite a pleasant little interlude and I couldn't help but be drawn into their seemingly impossible task.

'You are going to Turkey, yes?' Baptiste asked a short time later.

I accurately predicted the next question.

'Maybe you can give us a ride there?' He made it sound like we could just pop them down to the corner store, but Turkey was over 1,000 kilometres and many days' driving away. That would be like taking on boarders.

Mandy and I exchanged another quick telepathic glance. They had already espoused how they intended to siphon everything for free off everyone, an exceptionally poor lead-in to suggesting riding with your hosts for days on end. We were on a budget ourselves, one I had considered to be pretty tight till these guys reinvented the concept, so I certainly wasn't about to become a long-term hostel for wayward parasites. To escape this potential commitment, I suddenly found an out, spotting on our map a place which Mandy had previously raved about.

'Actually we are diverting, going to Meteora, monasteries in the mountains of Greece,' I explained, having now exhausted my entire knowledge on the topic. 'So look, we'll drop you off at the turnoff and if in a few days we are going through Thessaloniki, we'll text you.'

Their eyes betrayed the fact that they felt like they'd just lost a ride on a magic carpet to El Dorado.

When we reached the mountain junction in the late afternoon, it was snowing lightly. The kids launched out and threw snowballs at each other. Baptiste, Ulysses, Mandy and I did the same, exploding snow bombs on each other's heads. The boys then pulled their gear out, draped their useless plastic sheet over themselves and huddled down with their Thessaloniki sign. It was going to be dark soon and we hadn't seen another vehicle for some hours.

'What happens if you don't get a ride?' Mandy asked.

'Oh, we'll just sleep roadside.'

'Oh good, so you've got a winter tent and sleeping bags.' This made me feel better about deserting them here.

'No, just clothes.'

I shook my head as we launched back into the heated Franki. Their optimism was unbridled but they were quite simply the most ill-prepared pair of travellers I had ever met.

Mandy scanned the miserable sight of them in the snow with their plastic sheet and inappropriate clothing and then looked at me, like a baby harp seal. 'It's their journey,' I said defensively. 'They're not my responsibility! I've got enough kids.'

She waited. Harp seal eyes.

'Righto, righto,' I surrendered. 'They are sort of likeable. Open the larder, we're sponsors now.' I turned and called out the window, 'Why don't you guys come to Meteora with us?' I knew I'd regret this offer as I told them we'd be there a few days and then could drive them to Turkey. 'You can sleep under the awning in our sleeping bags. But in campgrounds, it'll be about three euros extra for you, so you will have to pay the extra fees.'

They had a man-huddle to discuss the offer. 'No thanks,' Baptiste eventually called back. 'Can't afford it. We'll keep going.'

It seemed the phrase 'pay the extra fees' was an anathema to them.

We passed them some more food and water as I felt an unnatural wave of concern roll over me. 'So where will you stay if you're not paying for hostels?' I asked.

'Oh, in big cities, we just approach people who look friendly and ask if they have somewhere we can sleep.'

I scratched my chin in pretend thoughtfulness, hoping that would camouflage my rampaging disbelief. 'Does that actually work?'

'Well, we don't know. We haven't actually done it yet.'

'I hope they're all right,' Mandy said as we disappeared over the mountain.

'Well, what can ya do? They think they're ten feet tall and bulletproof,' I replied.

I was secretly envious of their mad quest and youthful exuberance. Without kids, we may have joined them, but instead I found myself wondering if their parents would be worried. And then I began wondering if I was thinking like a parent. Oh my god! One minute we had been comparing Nirvana to the latest rap artist like BFFs and the next I was fretting over where they would sleep and who might take advantage of them. What was happening to me?

We drove through thick forest and across the Thessalian plains to reach Kalambaka at sunset. In Greek, Meteora literally meant 'suspended in the sky', and that best described the white monasteries that clung to the top of each towering mountain like specks of cream on the tip of giant sandstone fingers.

It seemed a ludicrous place to build anything. The location was remote and mostly uninhabited. But back in the twelfth century a bunch of hermit monks had spent a couple of hundred years building twenty-four monasteries here. Six remained. The only access to many of them had been by climbing into a net hitched over a hook which was then hand-winched across chasms. As a bonus, the monk occupants, stuck up in the towers like Rapunzel, ensured their piety would be protected because they could not be tempted to do anything but pray.

'A bit like Franki,' I laughed. 'We can't fall back into the temptations of our old life while we're remote from it.' Unfortunately I also knew that at some point we would have to reconnect with our old life and that prospect scared the hell out of me. To date, I had discovered no great theories as to how we could build a future that could be as simple, inspired and fun as this road lifestyle.

For two days we meandered from one needle-top monastery to another. I was repeatedly entertained by the orthodox monk rules which required my independent feminist wife and pretty feminist-in-training daughter to wear hideous one-size-fits-all long skirts, looking like perfect Amish women. Mandy hadn't worn a dress since our wedding, so failed to see the humour in my requests for her to fetch me a pail of water or knit a quilt.

By now, Baptiste and Ulysses' excellent adventure had captured our curiosity. We hoped that if our kids were one day travelling on a ridiculously stupid budget, some Griswold family in a motor home would adopt them for a few days. I sent them a text, offering the ride to Turkey and a reply came back almost instantly. I snickered. 'They must be hungry and sick of sleeping in fields by now.'

When we pulled into the Thessaloniki train station the following afternoon, they were waving ferociously at us.

'Prepare for the smell,' I warned, pinching my nose. As we stopped, they turned to a group of people and started hugging them. 'I don't remember them saying they knew anyone here,' I said.

'They didn't,' Mandy confirmed.

They happily bounced into the camper and we were immediately engulfed in a wave of fresh eau de cologne.

A pretty girl leant in the window, grabbed my hand and stared at me with tearful eyes. 'Look after them, please. They are good boys.' She then wistfully blew Ulysses a kiss.

I assured her we would, then turned and looked with suspicion at him, certain he had got more than just a free bed in Thessaloniki.

He shrugged and smiled happily back at me. We took off again and the lads proceeded to tell us how they had got a ride minutes after we'd left them at the top of the mountain. The driver had detoured into the centre of this city of over one million, and left them approaching people who 'looked friendly'.

'So what did you say to these friendly people?' I asked.

'Oh we just told them we were in the Rainbow group. Those guys,' he pointed out the window, 'had a spare house and gave us the keys.' Those same people had then brought them groceries and beer and shouted them out each night. The lads had been lounging in bubble-baths and sleeping in real beds, clearly not always alone, and their ten-euro capital outlay had remained untouched.

I started to think they were on to something with this Rainbow group thing.

As we drove on the long roads to the east past Alexandroupoli, we asked many questions. Apparently the first Rainbow gathering was held in America in 1972 and now pulls up to 30,000 people in countries all over the world. They set up in woodlands or forest and create a kind of temporary free community where no money is used to buy or sell anything. Sort of like a Woodstock without music. Their mantra is focused on peace. I had thought this hippy counterculture had died off with hitchhiking years ago.

We relaxed and drove on, debating all the great things the world could achieve if our leaders could stop draining us into the sinkhole with their insatiable obsession for re-election and economic growth at all cost. We were soon all slapping our thighs and raging against the machine, plucking our way through topics such as religion, Iraq, music, climate change and African famine, like a group of sixties students opposing Vietnam.

If I were still at work, I'd be dragged off to the company's counsellor if I spouted these views. But the great gift of travel was that I could be whoever I wanted, and today I was forever young, a university student plotting to save the world from greed, war, famine and environmental suicide.

Baptiste summarised the Rainbow gatherings. 'They allow people to pull the plug and have time out to look at themselves and listen to their quiet inner voices, to become spiritually aware and maybe find their true passion, beliefs or vocation.'

He had just defined our past nine months.

I was now embarrassed by my instant scepticism when we first picked up the lads. I had behaved like such a logical, realistic adult! My first thoughts when hearing of their quest was 'You can't do that', rather than seeing the magic in their great, impossible ambition.

Baptiste and Ulysses made me feel that anything was possible again. They reignited the free, hopeful spirit that drove me when I was twenty-three and backpacking, with little money, no job, no income, and no idea where I was going. By our new powers of telepathy, it was obvious that Mandy was also brimming with new inspiration.

The next afternoon we crossed into Turkey, watching with amusement as the guys argued with armed border guards about the compulsory fifteen-euro entry fee they considered outrageous. I tried suggesting that it wasn't in the traveller's code to antagonise armed militia but it stopped being funny when the guards decided to search our van as payback and we were delayed by hours.

We later dropped them off at a junction on the highway to Istanbul and this time it was a genuine detour. We were going south to the Gelibolu peninsula, Gallipoli.

'Do you think we should take out twenty or thirty euros from the bank for our month in Turkey?' Baptiste asked.

'I'd go with thirty,' I replied.

The kids had grown to enjoy the extra playful company in the back of the camper. They hugged Baptiste and Ulysses and we waved off our new-age Jack Kerouacs for the final time, off to save the world, armed with hope and a lot of dreams.

I figured the 'kids' who went to war and arrived at Gallipoli in 1915 were probably armed with the same great ambitions.

At the southern end of Anzac Cove, a concrete bunker lay blasted and crippled, tilted on an angle and lapping in the water, its sides pockmarked by bullets. I climbed into its claustrophobic cell, crouched down and peered through the narrow gun slot. In front of me panned the sparkling blue water of the Aegean Sea, a strip of sand, and the steep cliffs and ridges of green above. It was a beautiful setting, an ideal place for a resort – if it wasn't a cemetery reserve.

Peering through the bunker's slot was like viewing through an old camera, and soon my head was full of visions. I could see the boats landing over ninety years earlier in the morning mist. I could hear the 'whomp' of explosions and the bullets whistling around like 10,000 whipbirds. The first wave of 1,500 Allied troops was supposed to triumphantly sweep up the hills to Chunuk Bair with no resistance, but thousands of Turkish troops were huddled in wait. In the newsreel in my head, Aussie diggers jump out of the boats, hoping the breath they just took was not their last. They clamber for a small sand dune twenty feet from the water, just high enough to shield them from the shower of deadly metal raining down at an acute angle. The first arrivals press into the sand wall, pulling the next in closer. The ones four deep are exposed and being cut down, shrieking a death cry as their mates release their hands. These boys all become men before they ever stopped being boys.

I later joined Mandy and the kids and we climbed through the hillside trenches, the tiny distance between them so close the enemies could have almost lit each other's cigarettes. As we were there, a tour bus unloaded Turks into the trench opposite, and in a surreal re-enactment, I looked across the tiny divide into their eyes. Over 8,000 Aussies died here, but previously unknown to me, 80,000 Turks also died defending their homeland. Gallipoli was a hallowed place of pilgrimage for them too. From their trench, the Turkish group broke into broad grins, gave the thumbs up and cried, 'Aussie, Aussie, Aussie!' as though we were at a football game together.

They soon turned to go to the graveyards of their ancestors who were killed by mine. I turned to visit the graves of my people that were killed by theirs. And yet we have become friends.

At Lone Pine cemetery, gleaming white burial plaques stretch out across the manicured grass, vast numbers dating the lads that died on 25 April 1915 – Anzac Day. I had heard that Gallipoli could emotionally gut even the hardiest of souls, but I had not expected it to affect me. After all, I had no direct lineage to events here. But what sucked the breath from my lungs was the familiarity of the surnames in this distant place. Jones, McDonald, Foster, Smith. These names from my school class photos leapt up from the plaques, destroying any pre-conceived notion of mine that Gallipoli was a distant story about old men, told in black-and-white documentaries. It was about boys, like me and my mates had once been, who had gone off on an adventure of greatness with romantic recruitment promises to 'see the world' and 'meet French girls' – all wasted, all dead. To lie here in the soil. Forever young.

The final impact came when another long-buried memory exploded in my head. I am nine years old, swinging my arms and rushing to keep pace with my father. His World War II medals are pinned to my chest. I am saluting proudly as we march past the applauding Anzac Day crowds. My dad had been a private, a sapper. He died when I was seventeen. Cancer, the English language's worst word. I had adopted a lock-down mentality to get through the loss, and for over twenty-five years had successfully buried those memories with him, until now, when one particular headstone drew me into silence. It was the headstone of 845 Private Arthur Valentine Potter, 6th Battalion, Australian Infantry. Died 25 April 1915, age twenty. Its inscription said:

To live in hearts
We leave behind
Is not to die

Man, had I failed my father at that! The kids came running towards me yelling 'Daddy!' and I smiled at them through tears, knowing the power of travel had just helped me discover a magic new way of remembering my father with happiness. And I hoped with all my breath that, after I had gone, my kids would do the same.

As we left Gallipoli, we passed Atatürk's famous 1934 tribute he wrote for the Anzacs killed here, carved into rock at the landing beach. Its final lines stated:

You, the mothers, who sent their sons from far away countries
wipe away your tears; your sons are now lying in our bosom

and are in peace. After having lost their lives on this land they have become our sons as well.

The juxtaposition of our lives versus those past was never clearer. Here we were, meandering lazily with our children, from country to country, like rich colonials, but if we had been born in another time, or even another place right now, we could be fighting, starving or dead.

I had stopped wondering how Baptiste and Ulysses would survive, realising that whatever they'd do, however hard or ridiculous their actions might seem to others, at least they were doing it. With breath in their bodies, they had a real chance to find a new way. And for the first time since our journey began, I felt that we did too.

12

TURKISH RICHES

We had arrived in Turkey to find the country in the midst of a perfect storm that was destroying the financial lifeline tourism had been supplying them with. Kurdish militant groups had been setting off bombs in Istanbul and tourist areas – eight in recent months. Iraq was in disarray next door, Syria was constantly unsettled and another neighbour, Iran, had become America's focus for some serious sabre-rattling. And finally, the Western press was filled with stories of bird flu sweeping Europe, having originated from Doğubayazıt ('Doggy buys it' for the kids) in far-east Turkey. When I thought about all this, I started to wonder what we were doing here with kids.

My reservations increased when we pulled into Selçuk for a planned overnight stop and found the town's campsite was in the midst of reconstruction. The friendly owner insisted the hammering and sawing would be of little annoyance at 5 a.m., in fact they would cancel the project for the day just for us, this offer being an early sign that businesses were scrambling for any tourism income they could get.

But I did some quick guidebook scanning and was inspired by a description of a backpackers' place called Attila's that stated it had camping.

'A backpackers?' Mandy queried. 'What about the kids?'

It was a fair point. We may have wanted to be forever young, but our youth hostel days were past and these establishments weren't renowned as welcoming bastions for families. But it would be cheap, which we desperately needed. A previous stop at Çanakkale had included a quick email update. That was a mistake, reinforcing a strong argument for staying blissfully disconnected while on the road. We learnt that the tenants in our home had done a runner, leaving us thousands in the hole, our travelling money blasted.

On arrival at Attila's, the man himself greeted us with a rousing handshake while simultaneously looking at our motor home with a furrowed brow. He was half Australian and his family owned the hostel. 'Children?' he stammered, followed by, 'Camping?'

'Yeah, camping, it's in the guidebook.' I showed him the pages.

'Good description.' He smiled.

'Do you have power?' I asked.

'For what?'

It was obvious no one had ever arrived in a motor home before. 'Are you sure we won't be in the way with the kids?'

'Nah. No worries. You'll be right.' I now understood why Mandy cringed whenever I said that. 'Bring 'em in,' he assured us. 'This is Turkey.'

I didn't know what 'this is Turkey' was supposed to mean, but was certain he would say whatever it took to get our business.

He led us off the dusty road into the hostel's central courtyard. On entry we stopped abruptly and stared in wonderment like Dorothy's troupe looking down the yellow brick road. In front of us was an enchanted garden with fairy lights glittering through the lush trees. A lagoon swimming pool had water cascading into it and hammocks sprawled around it. Across the blue-lit waters sat a bamboo bar and a row of outdoor Turkish lounges, resplendent with colourful hangings, cushions and rugs.

'Forty lira,' Attila said. 'For all of you. Includes breakfast and dinner too.' I calculated it was cheaper than we could provide for ourselves. 'Happy hour has just started,' he went on. 'First drink is free. The beer's really cold. We'll set up a tab for you. Relax. My mum is a great cook. Dinner will be later.'

We sidled up to the bar and immediately suspected happy hour had been pretty happy for more than an hour. 'Is it OK for the kids to stay near the bar?' I asked Mick, a schoolteacher from remote Western Australia who had greeted us with a familiar drawled 'Gidday'.

'You're kidding?' he cried, and followed with that curious reasoning again. 'This is Turkey.'

There was then a rumbling noise like a stampede of small wildebeest coming up the stairs from the kitchen below. Attila's mum, aunty and other women swept out, waving their arms and rushing past us to scoop up our kids and land sloppy cheek kisses and bear hugs on them. And then I got it. Kids and family. This is Turkey.

With our children fostered out, we were suddenly off the leash and the first cold Efes beer flowed down the throat dangerously well. As the evening progressed, a load of young revellers arrived on the Fez bus, a hop-on, hop-off traveller's bus that circled the country. They swarmed the bar, rock music was pumped up. We shuffled off and put the kids to bed and did the responsible parent thing, taking turns to stumble from the bar to the van during the night to check that all the horrible noisy backpackers weren't disrupting the children's sleep. We hadn't been out at night for months, handcuffed to Franki. By midnight, we were wearing knitted Rasta caps, ticking away repeatedly at the bar tab, sucking on fruit-flavoured shisha pipes and screeching away to INXS, Meatloaf and AC/DC's 'You Shook Me All Night Long'.

We cancelled our transit plans the next morning.

Selçuk was on the map as it was next to Ephesus, reputed to be one of the best preserved ancient cities in the east Mediterranean and containing the Temple of Artemis, one of the seven ancient wonders of the world. Barman Jeff insisted I had to see it, but I resisted, stating I had just seen Troy.

'Oh Troy!' he groaned. 'Ignore that shithole!'

The highlight of our visit to Troy the day before had been to play inside the giant wooden horse that replicated the one that cunning old Greek warrior Odysseus used to end the legendary Trojan War. Later, when I dragged the kids out of the grand toy horse on a promised cultural exploration of great ruins, all we found were just that – ruins. And as ruins go, Troy was completely ruined.

Mandy refused to leave the trove of English books she had discovered in reception and the kids were ruin-shy and happy for a day of stillness. So at Jeff's repeated insistence, I went to Ephesus alone.

Ephesus was obviously once a pretty popular place and not just because Efes beer was named after it. It was filled with preserved sections of marble streets, fountains, temples, intricate frescoes and mosaics. There were small theatres, prisons and brothels as well as a large 25,000-seat amphitheatre. The library was most impressive, a preserved two-storey façade with columns and statues. Ruins were back on my list.

I arrived back at Attila's later, after devouring the world's greatest kebab, to find the children had taken over one of the Turkish lounges, building their own cities with blocks, backgammon and okey pieces. 'Go away, Daddy,' was my welcome. Every stuffed toy they owned was placed around, amphitheatre-style, and during the afternoon they held court to a procession of visitors including Attila's extended family, the chef, Carlos the bus driver, Rebecca the barmaid, Jeff, a smattering of guests and the guy who ran reception who never spoke to anyone but became simply garrulous around the kids.

'It would seem,' I observed to Mandy, 'that we, their nurturers and protectors, are old hat.'

She looked up from her fourth book of the day. 'We have a dozen babysitters here, babe. We don't have to cook or clean. We don't have to think about where we stay tomorrow, or how to get there. I get cold drinks delivered to my deck chair. The kids haven't stopped giggling all day. This place is Club Med. We're never leaving. Now go away.'

Comprehensively rejected by my family, I joined Mick and the Mayor of Selçuk at the bar for happy two hours and the night followed the same rambunctious pathway as the one before. We departed Attila's five days later, the kids more popular in a backpackers than I had ever been.

It was the dazzling pearly white sand of Ölüdeniz on the south coast that eventually lured us away. The waterfront campsite was again more like a resort, but in peak season, the place was almost empty. The manager blamed the American president for changing the world and trying to start wars.

'Is it also the bird flu?' I asked, aware of the coverage this apparently imminent human apocalypse was getting in the popular press around the world.

'What bird flu?' he replied.

The colourful beanbags set around the beach provided the ideal setting for relaxation but I was quickly reminded that travelling with kids retained a certain edge. I was lying around reading. Mandy was having a long shower. The iPod was playing Jimmy Buffet. The children were outside in the dirt. And then boom! We were on Defcon alert.

Callum and Jaimie both started screeching in the real panic tones I could now recognise instantly. I launched up to find Callum on the ground, hyperventilating. Jaimie was adjacent, screaming and pointing hysterically at him.

'What? What!' I yelled, desperately looking around for a snake, a scorpion or a nest of green ants.

Mandy had burst from the shower and arrived panting in a towel. But Callum was apoplectic, pointing at his foot. I grabbed it, sweeping and slapping at it, till I found a tiny black ant between his toes. I brushed it off and he ceased yelling as though a light had been flicked off. By this time we were surrounded by every person within a one-kilometre radius.

'The ant walked on him, Daddy,' Jaimie explained.

'Not bitten? He... walked... on you?' I repeated in disbelief.

'Yes. Gone now.'

I smiled up dopily at the wagon wheel of people who had all charged over to help avert this disaster, knowing then that I should have strapped that Moroccan peacock to the roof.

After Ölüdeniz, we wound around the spectacular southern coastline to Kas, once a place of exile for political dissidents and now a bohemian hangout. The town's campsite was near a coliseum ruin and we could jump directly into the crystal blue ocean from Franki's porch. We hadn't eaten out since being in Italy, so decided to strap in for a long lunch even though our budget was now on life support. We chose a restaurant near the boat harbour as it had the particular benefit of being on a square that was full of birds the kids could chase. Our waiter arrived quickly. 'Hello, welcome, my name is Ekrem.'

As had become custom in every conversation we had in Turkey, we asked about the other person's respective family, children, ages, names and homes. Ekrem, like many other young Turkish guys, was disarming with his openness. 'Yes, I would like to have children, very important, but it is hard to meet the right girl and save for her and first I must contribute to my family. My sister needs the money as her husband just died.'

The restaurant owner, the chef and the adjoining shop owner all came out to kiss our children, touch their hair and offer them gifts of water balloons to toss at the birds. Ekrem rang his sister who ran puffing down the street at the news that two little kids were here. We talked about Australia, Turkey and families and nodded sagely about how threats of war were ruining business and the world. As the afternoon mellowed away, we consumed Efes beers and a bottle of wine, the budget genie flown. We ate fish, kebab meat and Turkish bread, the kids flocking back to the table like seagulls whenever there was food on it. Ekrem continued to recharge our glasses, but on one occasion, stopped, turned to me and said slowly with great emphasis, 'You are a very rich man!'

I froze, instantly panicking about the cost of this meal splurge. My mind raced. I must have stuffed up on the conversion and spent a fortune. Or maybe he had been friendly just to scam money from us. The mere fact I could even be here with my family made me wealthy in this country, even if we were on what we considered a meagre allowance. 'Oh I don't know about that,' I replied, embarrassed.

'No, no!' He continued his crazed stare. 'You are a very, very rich man.'

'We-ellll,' I drawled, hoping to escape this conversation.

'Look!' Ekrem waved his arm towards the fountain where Jaimie and Callum were squealing with laughter. 'You have two very beautiful children.' His r's kept rolling. 'Look at them. Look!'

I looked.

'A boy and a girl. Healthy and happy,' he continued. 'I tell you. You are as rich as a man can be.' And off he walked.

I kept looking. My recent thoughts had been dominated by the loss of our rent money and yet this Turkish waiter had reminded me that I had been deceiving myself, again, worrying about things of no real importance. What he didn't realise, though, was that I was also looking at my wife. Her eyes were crinkling up in the way I loved when she laughed at her own jokes, funny or not. I had spent a lot of time on this journey reflecting on my absent relationship with my kids and yet it suddenly became blindingly obvious that I was richer still for having this soul mate and life-explorer, Mandy, at my side. To me, she was the glue that bound the four of us. As I sat there with a goofy smile on my face, I remembered reading about a nanny giving advice to a harassed modern mother of two. 'Remember,' she had said, 'before they got here, it was just the two of you. When they're gone, it'll be just the two of you.'

We hadn't yet entered the whirlpool of school, sleepovers, sports, and lessons for piano, Mandarin and violin. I could not say what we would do when the children's demands started to swell, but I had seen the path other couples had slid off and it was a scary descent. A decade and a half of them becoming glorified taxi drivers, and sacrificing themselves to create perceived perfect childhoods, while they floated away from each other like two land masses in a continental drift. It may be selfish, particularly in this age when the mere suggestion that children are not one's main focus can cause uproar, but I knew I had to prioritise future energies into 'the two of us', my wife and I, foremost, and 'the four of us' would hopefully prosper in our wake.

I stood up and hugged Ekrem, an activity I rarely do with waiters. 'Thank you. You are a very wise man,' I said, rolling my r's. 'And I... am a very rich one.'

We continued on the 'circuit', the backpacker trail that led us to the ruins of the ancient city of Olympos and the domain of international backpackers where the bulk of the accommodation comprised timber treehouses. We were given a spot to park out the back of one such treehouse establishment and were presented with a power cable and a thirty-lira all-inclusive bill. A bunch of travellers we had met over the previous weeks arrived on boat cruises from Fethiye and the nightly parties started all over again, including a disco in a nearby coliseum ruin. And each day, the kids were feted as royalty by staff and visitors who played with them or showered them with small gifts and treats. Through them, we were meeting more people and learning more about the local culture from a completely different angle than when travelling solo or without kids.

With the waiter Ekrem's words of richness still fresh, I knew I would do anything to protect this 'wealth'. I just didn't know then how soon this test would come. Many driving days after Olympos, over mountains and deserts, through a snowstorm, rain, shimmering heat, and an instantaneous diarrhoea bout that made me appreciate the on-board conveniences of Franki more than ever, we were deep inside a narrow gorge at Belisirma in the Ihlara Valley in central Turkey. We had come here to see the hundreds of old caves and churches from the Middle Ages that honeycombed the cliff walls. We were the lone camper in the gorge, parked in the backyard of a restaurant. A stream, the Melendiz Suyu, flowed past. It was dark, lush and cool in the canyon, like a lost world.

But during the night, heavy rain swirled around the van like a car wash. I climbed out to pull in the flapping awning and splashed into water inches deep. It was a terrifying discovery. The Melendiz's waters had risen impossibly fast and were now booming through the gorge. Television news images of flash floods, where people and villages were washed away and killed in faraway places like... well... Turkey, instantly tore through my mind.

'Flash flood!' I reported back to Mandy. 'We have to get out!' But the one causeway exit was now an impassable raging torrent. I ran in the opposite direction up the gorge and found another restaurant with a raised parking area. I judged it was our only hope. 'I will try and bring our camper here,' I called to the owner through the horizontal rain as he was rescuing his tables from the river torrent.

'Where is it now?' he yelled back.

'Behind that other restaurant!'

'Yes, yes do that! Bring it quick! Much better here!'

Water was seeping over the river banks and beginning to submerge our site. The time to get out was almost gone. Mandy secured the kids' bed barriers before I ploughed Franki through the watery driveway, lumbering slowly forward into the sodden tracks like a drugged elephant. The van slowed and slewed but in its last breath of momentum, the front tyres reached up onto the road and we drove to the higher ground.

Our new host, Abdullah, placed us dripping wet around a wood-burning stove.

'What do we do now?' I asked him.

'We wait,' Abdullah replied.

He seemed unnaturally calm in the face of certain destruction. 'But what about the flash flood?'

'Flash flood?' he cried, and then rocked back in laughter. 'No, no, my friend,' he continued. 'This happens all the time. They open up the dam at the top of the gorge when there's too much water. This is as high as it will get. I am afraid, my friend, you have not saved your family today,' he laughed, slapping me on the back.

'Why didn't you tell me that when I ran up to you in the rain?'

'Are you kidding?' he bellowed. 'You just tore up my cousin's yard with your van and brought your business to me!'

Turkish entrepreneurs; they would do anything for business. The two cousins were still arguing over our night fee when we left.

Göreme was the capital of Cappadocia. Isolated in the desert, it was an other-world scene of caves, pinnacles and small rock mountains condensed into a tiny village. Modern traffic and colourful air balloons moved through the landscape in a surreal contrast to the rocky prehistoric setting. Our campground was located in a group of fairy chimneys. These erect rock formations were difficult to describe but I gave it my most eloquent shot. 'We are camped among giant penises,' I wrote to my mum.

Restaurant and cave bar owners offered to babysit or play kids' movies, or just sat around and, like Ekrem, told us how blessed we were to have two such children. When we went to the underground city of Derinkuyu, a local schoolteacher insisted he climb down the eight storeys into the earth with us, just so he could play tour guide to the kids. He told them how these underground cities dated back 4,000 years to the Bronze Age, housing entire populations from invading armies. The underground beehives included tunnels, stores, wineries, homes, stables, churches and mills. A hundred of his schoolchildren swarmed over our van as we left, just to present our kids with two handmade dolls.

Police would pull us over, to check out the van and practise English, but once they discovered the kids on board, they would rush off and return with their wives and own children, bringing food, tea and gifts. These initially intimidating roadblocks became so enjoyable, we got to the point where we were disappointed when we weren't pulled over by the police.

Overall it seemed that having a camper in Turkey was unique, being Australian cemented a kinship borne of Gallipoli, and having kids endeared us.

Before we departed on this trip, I expected our travels would be different with children. It would include sacrifice, cost and frustration, but I never envisaged how much richer it could be.

We really knew the Turkish tourism business was tough when we passed through the town of Kahta on the way to see the famed mountaintop statues of Nemrut Dagi.

We were powering on after two constant driving days east, aware of being only a few hundred kilometres from the Iraq and Iran borders in the middle of Kurdish territory. Being kidnapped or blown up wasn't on our agenda.

As we left town, a car filled with robed men came racing up beside us, the driver blasting the horn, the other men waving frantically and pointing to our tyres.

'Keep going,' I said to Mandy.

But they kept at us until finally we pulled over, entertaining the possibility there was something wrong with the van. One man ran up to my window while Mandy kept the van in gear, ready to roar off at any sign of danger.

'Mister! Missus! Hello!' The toothless man brandishing a fistful of brochures cried. 'We were on the roof of the hotel watching for tourists through binoculars and saw you coming across the plains.'

Did that sound as desperate to him as it did to me? 'You can't get to see the statues and heads,' he cried. 'The roads are washed out and too steep for your wonderful vehicle. You must take a tour. I can do. Cheap! You stay at my family's hotel!'

It was more an order than an offer, but our scam radar was on, so we thanked him for the advice and drove off with his insistent warnings ringing in our ears.

The roads were fine and we camped one night on the lower side of Mount Nemrut, and then crawled up 2,000 metres to within twelve kilometres of the summit, camping in the back of a small pension.

Our new host, Imman, was far more trustworthy than Kahta's desperate road crew. He even said so himself. 'Trust me, there is absolutely no way you can get to the top in a large seven-berth motor home,' he assured. 'I arrange a car and driver cheap for you.'

Mandy was sure he too was scamming us, but this time I disagreed. She relented and we paid a sum equivalent to twenty euros, an extravagant amount for such a short journey in Turkey. We were then driven at sunset the final kilometres to the peak, our chauffeured, rattling car making hard work of the sharp switchbacks and cobbled road, until it pulled in at the top, parking next to a large seven-berth motor home.

The final section to the peak was up a steep path over a strange mound of thousands of fist-sized rocks of white limestone, sitting as a cone on top of the mountain. It's believed the statues and stones were placed here as a burial mound of King Antiochus I, dating back to 62 BC.

We crossed around to the western terrace for sunset where the iconic cluster of Nemrut Dagi's giant heads and statues were lined up. Some remained standing tall and proud, their profiles featuring prominent noses and bushy beards. There were lions and eagles and others that represented famed deities like Apollo, Zeus and Hercules. Some had crumpled noses or had fallen and lay on the ground. These monuments would have filled museums the world around but here they lay like broken rubbish, on the top of a mountain in the middle of nowhere, weathering away in snow and sun each year.

We sat and watched as the statues' details changed through a myriad of glowing orange, yellow and red hues as the sun fell out of the sky. There was a small straggle of tourists on the peak, most from other parts of Turkey, but I particularly noticed the Western family with two young kids. These were the only other foreign children we had seen in Turkey and were obviously from the motor home below, so I struck up a conversation.

They were French and had been circumnavigating the globe, having been to Alaska, North and South America, New Zealand, Australia, India, the Middle East, and now here. They shipped their machine everywhere and had home-schooled their two kids, now aged eight and ten.

I was mightily impressed. 'Four years! They're like the grand pooh-bahs of travelling families,' I whispered to Mandy, hardly able to get my head around such a long time on the road with kids. I was also curious as to what they did that enabled this lifestyle. Travel writers? Independently wealthy? Crash payout recipients? Maybe they had just said, 'Fuck it,' and were spending every cent they had. I couldn't ask them because I had banned the 'what do you do' question from all conversations. But it didn't really matter and I didn't really care. The thing was they had decided to live a life less ordinary.

Yet this almost ludicrous concept of four years travelling triggered a chemical release in my little brain. Could we do that? How good would that be? Could we just keep on keeping on? What if? It sounded hard. But maybe it was the answer I had long been searching for.

They'd clearly created a lifestyle out of their adventure, not just a temporary breakaway, and I was suddenly entranced by new possibilities and the reward of a family bonding that would last the ages like the figures atop Mount Nemrut. 'We have to change everything, not take the easy path and fall back into our old way of life,' I declared that night. 'We have to continue the voyage... somehow.'

From Nemrut Dagi, we did continue our voyage, a large return loop over many lazy days towards Istanbul. Once there, we visited Istanbul's old town, Sultanahmet, numerous times over a number of days. It was packed with ostentatious buildings, ancient churches and the city's signature features: the Blue Mosque, with its soaring minarets and imposing dome; and the grand bazaar with its 4,000-odd shops. The Topkapi Palace, the home of sultans past, was also a must-see, where Mahmud III had prominently stocked his harem with over 300 concubines, producing a hundred kids. In the palace's treasury was the jewel-encrusted skull and hand of St John the Baptist – an item I was most ebullient about until I later discovered there are other such encrusted St John hands in Montenegro, Mount Athos, West Bengal, Bulgaria and Egypt. It was a miracle, I thought. St John was an octopus.

Istanbul's nearest campground was hidden away off a thundering road behind a BP service station. Sitting next to us in the grassed enclosure was an impressively kitted out Toyota Land Cruiser with a tent on its roof and a sticker on its rear that read 'One life… live it!'

This inevitably drew us to Lizzie and Rohl, a young Dutch couple who had sold everything they owned to drive to Australia from Holland via the Middle East and Africa. I stalked around their vehicle, inspecting the fit-out and questioning them at length, still fermenting a new quest that could keep us going forever.

One afternoon I crossed the thumping highway and reluctantly checked our emails. I came back and reported the news. Our car, which we had lent out, had been smashed up and wrecked. One friend's kid had a brain haemorrhage and another friend had just been diagnosed with terminal cancer at forty-two. I looked across at the 'one life' sticker again. Our budget may have taken a hit, but with our kids and health, our wealth was extreme. And four years away was making even more sense.

13

TRAPPED IN EASTERN EUROPE

A remote border outpost exists high up in the thickly forested Strandzha Mountains, iced up and impassable for months of the year. In communist times this was apparently a sensitive crossing between Turkey and Bulgaria. It didn't look like much had changed since. A guard was squeezed inside a small booth that perched outside a crumbling and pockmarked concrete building. He was wearing a furry hat and holding a gun. He saw the kids but they did not melt him, so I dispensed with unwanted pleasantries and diligently compiled every possible document this guard might request. We passed over our passports, the vehicle registration, 'car lease agreement', letters of ownership and finally the green card, the vital proof of vehicle insurance required by law.

The little man in the booth started scanning through all the papers in an overly officious manner. Bulgaria had not yet entered the EU, so he was clearly the big fish in this little pond. I waited to hear the beautiful sound of the 'thump' of rubber stamps into our passports, but as minutes passed, the furrow on his brow deepened. Eventually he slid open the window and barked out, 'No insurance!'

'Ya, ya.' I pointed to the green papers in a sycophantic fashion, the only way to treat a border guard with a big furry hat and an automatic weapon.

'No insurance!' he spat and threw the papers back in the car. 'Go there!' he jerked his arm towards the decrepit concrete building.

'What is this dickhead talking about?' I mumbled to Mandy. 'He obviously can't read.'

Mandy was forced to reverse away from the boom gate to let the one lone waiting car through as I skipped through the papers that I had never actually read before. As I did, my face slowly turned white. 'Ohhhh shit!'

'What?'

'The insurance,' I stammered. 'It expired last week. We have no insurance.'

Silence filled the cabin. This was a big deal. No country would let us enter without insurance, hence there was no way we could pass through the three more border crossings ahead to get back into the non-existent border world of the EU.

'How could that be?' she snatched the papers off me. 'We paid for twelve months.'

'Yeah I know that, but look at the expiry date.' I pointed. 'Donna only did ten months.'

'Oh my god. Why would she do that?'

Temperatures were rising. 'How the hell would I know?'

'What do we do?'

I knew my family needed me to be a pillar of calm strength so I adopted my fix-all approach – I bopped my head repeatedly into the dash, muffled obscenities and wished a plague of locusts to descend upon Donna, her relatives, her pets and her crops. The kids, meanwhile, leant back in their chairs trying to get as far away from me as their seatbelts would allow.

'Right!' I psychotically declared, having exorcised that demon. 'We're hundreds of miles from nowhere, in some scene from *Spies Like Us*, with no insurance, no petrol and mink-hatted guards with big guns and bigger attitudes. We can't go backwards because we have no fuel, and if we did we would simply have to sit in Turkey waiting weeks for papers and miss the World Cup!' Germany's football World Cup had become somewhat of a holy grail for the sports-mad me over recent months. 'There's only one thing to do.'

'I don't think we can run this border, Johnny,' Mandy said.

'Nooo. We play the stupid tourist Australians, then beg, then bribe. Look at these guys. They've been brought up in a world of graft and backhanders,' I said as though I knew these things.

'That's your plan? Bribe border guards?'

'Yes! After stupidity and begging. No worries.'

I stuffed some US dollars into my socks, left the family, and entered the building ready to implement my brilliant three-pronged plan. After a long wait, I got to a window to be told I was in the wrong line. I looked around to see another manned window. As I moved towards it, the woman slid it closed for lunch.

By this time the family had either got bored waiting or was curious to see if I had been arrested. Jaimie entered and held my hand. Callum supported our crisis by screaming up a storm, which echoed loudly off the concrete walls and linoleum floors. For once I was happy to have him in full voice as this helped us get attention. We were eventually hustled into a private office, although this is never a good sign at a border crossing.

I sat Jaimie on my lap and smiled at the official like a moronic ventriloquist with his dummy. He ignored us and munched slowly through a sub-sized sandwich, spraying crumbs through his beard. Eventually he wiped his mouth and finished. 'Your insurance expired.' He tapped our green card.

'Is it?' My eyes bulged. Plan A – stupid, was in action. 'No. Not possible. We pay for one year. See!' I pointed to the start date.

'Expire!' He pointed to the end date. Damn it, he could read.

'Oh my god! I do not understand!' And on I waffled, the perfect idiot, which I would later be advised was merely playing to my strengths.

He sat staring and uncaring. He was not going to let us in. I could see my dreams of going to the World Cup slipping away. I reverted to Plan B – begging. 'But my children, my family,' I whined. 'Where will we sleep? We have no petrol,' I wailed on, sounding more like Oliver Twist. 'Please, sir!'

He just stared, not appreciating what I considered a sterling performance.

Then finally the opportunity I was searching for cracked open. 'Unless,' he said thoughtfully.

It was a beautiful word, 'unless'. I touched the American dollars in my socks. Plan C – bribery. 'Ya, ya, unless what?' I leant forward conspiratorially.

'Unless you buy our insurance,' he said.

I smiled at this code speak for cash in his pocket.

'Yes, ya.' I winked. 'Your insurance. I understand.' I pulled the small wad of cash out of my shoe and started flicking notes like a cheap Vegas gambler paying off a hooker. 'How much for you, my friend... to make this problem go away?'

He stared at me. He was very good at that. 'Over there,' he said. 'You can buy Bulgaria insurance for seven days – thirty-five euros. It is transit only. You must leave before it expires or you will be here illegal.'

Had I been able to read Bulgarian I would have worked this out some hours ago. I was actually quite disappointed that it was all above board. Bribery seemed so much more romantic. 'But how do I get into Serbia then? Do they also sell insurance?'

He shrugged. 'Serbia, who knows?'

I sat back and absorbed this. At least this thirty-five euros would get us across the border but delay the problem to another day.

'OK, good,' I said, fixing the problem for now. 'One more thing. Where is the fuel station? We are empty.'

'Next town. Malko Tarnovo. Maybe open. You will need Bulgaria cash, lev, to pay.'

'OK. Where is cash machine? We have no lev.'

'Malko Tarnovo. Maybe working. Maybe not.'

'Tourist maps?' I squeaked in hope.

'No.' He shook his head sideways again.

After paying thirty-five euros for seven days' insurance, we were back at the hut facing our nemesis guard and his boom gate barrier. The little bureaucrat now held our papers up to the light as though looking for counterfeits or another reason to decline us. He finally sighed, slammed stamps into our passports and looked deeper into the van at the children. 'Ah ha!' he cried. 'You have beautiful children!'

I was sideswiped by his demeanour change, but replied by putting my hand over my heart, and with a slight forward nod of the head, replied in a broken accent that rolled the r's heavily, 'Yes, we are very rich!'

His eyebrows arched upwards in surprise at my reply. He nodded, opened the boom gate and off we roared.

For the next fifty metres at least. We were then halted at another boom gate where we had to pay a five-euro 'road use' tax and a four-euro 'disinfection tax', the latter involving a de-lousing of Franki by a chap with a chemical spray gun. Unfortunately, I was outside at the time paying the road tax and got personally disinfected as well.

He eventually opened the boom and off we finally roared into the freedom of Bulgaria, with no fuel, no cash, no maps and no way out.

Like the rugged ancient forest we were driving through, Malko Tarnovo appeared frozen in another era. Utilitarian concrete buildings in various states of repair lined the streets. I was almost expecting Marxist guards to come marching round the corner. We parked and I went in search of directions to a fuel station. The place was eerily silent. A few window curtains peeped open and I could sense a hundred eyes watching my every step. A shop that sold the latest fashion – disco clothes from the seventies – was open, but I was soon gruffly pointed back out onto the streets where a few mangy dogs circled around.

Surprisingly, the town's one cash machine worked, and eventually two pasty overweight teenager girls in seventies kit with technicolour hair, high boots and shrapnel through their faces, gave me sign language directions to a fuel station. On the way there we ran out of fuel but were able to roll the last few hundred feet downhill.

After the long, stressful border crossing, we were all eager to move on. I waved around a brochure of the campground at Sozopol that promised a Club Med camper park. I was up-selling to get the mood in the camper back up. 'It's a Slavic paradise!' I emphasised the c with a spitting cough because I liked saying words that ended in c in Eastern Europe and the kids thought it was funny. 'And beaches to die for.'

We cruised along the Black Sea and arrived at the richly described campsite at dusk. Mandy was exhausted from a long driving day that started before dawn and was still worried about the insurance hanging over us. A swim was needed. Mandy turned off the engine and we all just sat there staring at the camp gates in disbelief.

Franki was surrounded by a thousand crystals of broken glass. The rusted gates were secured by a rustier padlock. The reception building was boarded up, although most of its windows were broken. The grass behind the barbed wire fence was six feet high. I got out and wandered around as Mandy slumped at the wheel. I found a yard keeper, although I'm not sure what he was keeping. Our clashing languages eventually established that the park was closed, for those who hadn't worked that out. I showed him the opening dates in the guidebook but that wasn't about to get the place mown and renovated in the next ten minutes. We had no intention of bush camping as Bulgaria had a dubious reputation for tourist safety, so we continued our search for my promised Slavic paradise.

Our final resting place for the night was more like an elephant's graveyard of disused caravans, but it had two things going for it: it was open and we had no choice. Most of the caravans were sunk up to their floors in the sand and leant at varying angles from the buffeting of the winds.

The next day we wandered around Sozopol, spending hours trying to call and email Donna, our van person in Utrecht, to find out about the green card. Internet was down and telephones weren't working. Eventually, after I reignited my three-prong strategy, playing dumb, begging and offering money, the town's best hotel let me use their fax machine. By afternoon, I had made contact with Donna.

'Oh yes!' she happily cried. 'I have had your insurance renewal certificate here for some time. I was waiting for you to contact me so I could send it somewhere.'

I was dumbstruck. Was I a fucking mind reader? 'You said it was for twelve months!' I cried.

'Oh, yes, well I just did it for ten months, as it matched the date on my other cars and that meant I didn't have to go to the post office twice. Must have forgotten to tell you.' She laughed.

'Uh huh.' I was befuddled by her omission of this slightly important fact, but realised that a tirade wasn't going to help as we were now totally reliant on her couriering the documents to us fast. I also figured I was somewhat complicit in all this for not having ever checked the papers.

'Bulgaria?' she asked. 'Gee, that's a bad place to post to. Could take weeks!' She guffawed again.

We finally arranged to have the card sent to the American Express office in Bulgaria's capital, Sofia, making that our new next destination. All we could now do was hope it would arrive within a few days as we didn't want to be stuck in this country for too long. 'Good luck,' was Donna's final supportive sign-off.

We spent another day sitting in the sand dunes watching tractors trawl along the beach, moving mountains of seaweed and dead fish and dumping down white sand to make it look good for the tourist season. Concrete monstrosities fronted the beach. These were being built by developers and sold by their persuasive English sales agents as a Black Sea paradise. Maybe we were there at the wrong time, but paradise it was not.

We decided not to make our entire visit to Bulgaria about an insurance card. With four days left on our transit insurance, we left the beach and drove through the spectacular central Bulgarian countryside, detouring north to traipse around the old ancient capital of Veliko Tarnovo. It was a fortress town that sat perched on a hill surrounded by rivers and valleys.

After Franki stopped working for a mystery period when we were camped in a remote area near the Dryanovo Monastery and Bacho Kiro cave, the decision was made to drive non-stop to the capital Sofia, where we could get help if she didn't start again.

On the way, adjacent to one petrol station was a kids' play area. 'A playground, a playground,' the kids squealed once their radar had picked up on it.

'Sorry, we have to keep going. But no worries, the campground has a great playground. Here, look at the brochure.' I passed them a four-page colour brochure of the Sofia campsite that inspired little 'ooohs' and 'aaahs'.

We arrived at campsite Vrana at sunset. It was ten kilometres from the centre of Sofia city and we were again excited about relaxing in a well-equipped campground that was so beautifully laid out in its brochures. Once again, however, Bulgaria proved better at marketing than reality.

We should have recognised this trend to mislead by the content of the roadside billboards throughout the country. If a billboard didn't have a nude girl on it, or at least one in a G-string holding her breasts, then I don't think the advertisers were serious about selling their product. There were girls cooling themselves in front of air conditioners or getting their gear off while eating a Bulgarian breakfast cereal called Fitness. Petrol, supermarkets, casinos, gymnasiums, dog food, cell phones – it seemed that just about any consumer item in this country created an uncontrollable urge that made women want to strip and grab their own breasts.

'It's disgusting, using women as objects like that!' Mandy observed. 'The only time a guy is on a billboard,' she went on, 'is when he is standing leering behind a girl. You can't see his bum or anything!'

At Vrana, we were escorted through the site by a heavily pregnant dog and a chain-smoking receptionist, a tall ageing peroxide blonde with a fake tan. She led us to a patch of grass that had been mown, in contrast to the rest of the campground. Behind us was an overgrown laneway leading to some dilapidated cabins, one of which we were instructed to use for showers, with the caveat, 'if they work'. We later found the beautiful restaurant in the brochure, but it was so overgrown with vines it looked more like the temples of Angkor Wat. The campsite's brochure was so dramatically misleading that I now felt the billboards were more realistic in suggesting people were driven to nudity while eating breakfast cereal.

'At least it's open,' Mandy optimistically pointed out.

The kids were not as happy, though. 'But you promised there would be a playground, Daddy!'

There were two days left on our temporary Bulgarian insurance. The next morning, no amount of coaxing could get Franki started. Mandy also made a curious observation. 'Did you notice the lights of cars coming through to the cabins behind us during the night?'

'Nope, didn't see or hear anything.'

'Coming and going every few hours?'

'No idea,' I said before heading off to see if Donna had in fact sent our insurance papers to the Sofia Amex office. I walked out on to the highway to flag down a minibus, the prevailing public transport system. As I stood there, an exceptionally cute girl in scantily clad clothing and bright red hair started jabbering at me in Bulgarian. I replied, 'No sprechens en Bulgarian,' hoping that made sense.

She tried again and got the same unintelligible response from me. Clearly exasperated, she pointed to my groin and made a 'sucking the lollipop' motion in and out of her mouth.

'Oh!' I finally twigged to what was going on. 'No, nyet, thanks. No for me.' I held up my hands.

Recognising English, she adapted quickly. 'Sex?' and started motioning downhill skiing before pointing to the cabins in the campground as a suitable venue for such a dalliance. I realised that Mandy's observation of night-time taxis now made sense. I replied negatively again. The girl finally patted my arm and smiled sadly as though knowing I had missed out on something special. She then wiggled off down the highway with me admiring both her bottom and her succinct ability to communicate in sign language.

So there we stood on the side of the highway, 100 metres apart, both waving our hands trying to get a ride, of sorts. I watched as cars pulled up and she leant in, negotiating. On one occasion, a large heavily tinted black vehicle stopped, and then crawled down to where I was standing. A big bald man zapped the window down, smiled and started playing the lollipop game with me.

I took it as a compliment that a fat, sweaty Bulgarian thought I was attractive enough to take his manhood into my mouth, but I quickly invented my own not-so-subtle sign language to indicate I was not offering this alternative.

I returned later with no documents to find the pregnant mongrel dog had had puppies under Franki and they were urinating all over our patch of grass. Two days later, our Bulgarian insurance expired and so, for the second time in our journey, we were breaking the law in a foreign country. We could not approach the border, even if Serbia sold transit insurance, because Bulgaria would fine us first. We were trapped in Eastern Europe.

Franki's on-again, off-again starting problem was diagnosed as a broken glow plug. Our friendly local mechanic, who was actually a moonlighting hairdresser, replaced it after a few days of trial and error.

I was very down about missing the World Cup. Mandy suggested I fly to Germany and she would catch up. 'You'll only get one chance,' she argued. She tried to make it easy on me. 'And anyway, I have no interest in going to some stupid football tournament where there will be massive crowds. The kids won't like it. You go.'

There may have been a time when I would have leapt on this offer, but I couldn't leave her here with the kids in this brothel of a campsite, and even if I could get past that, I had no desire to. This odyssey had become all about our little clan. If they couldn't come, I wouldn't go. I had no idea when this family focus took over – somewhere on the road, somewhere among the events we shared and the lessons I was learning. I finally resigned myself to missing out on the World Cup.

And in that resignation I started to make the best out of our Bulgarian imprisonment in this squalor of a campsite. Each day, one or all of us travelled into the city and came back empty-handed. We took the kids to the movies to see *Shaggy Dog* and stuffed our faces with McDonald's and ice cream. Mandy and I took turns at having big days out. Jaimie and Callum spent their days running around the campsite in rubber boots and playing football in the grass. We lit fires at night because there didn't appear to be any rules. We entertained ourselves by counting taxis and noting large Bulgarian men with amenable girls arriving at all hours of day and night.

Time slid quietly into June.

The strange thing was that with the winds blowing against us, we were having a great time together. Before the trip, the thought of just hanging out for days on end with Mandy and the kids would have made me shiver but now I was wallowing in it. Kicking footballs, playing chasey through the woods or cooking the meals together. The kids played in their own world while Mandy and I read books, scratched away at Sudoku, drank wine under the stars, philosophised about saving the world, or did whatever 'project' was the centrifugal force of the day. It was the best worst campsite I've ever stayed in.

But after a week of transiting in and out of Sofia and sticking my imaginary Donna doll with pins for the green card stuff-up,

I lost patience. 'Let's take our chances on the border without insurance. Who cares if they fine us hundreds of euros? We've gotta get outta here! We're running out of time before we go home.'

I hadn't meant to say it, but the verbalisation of the word 'home' landed between us like a mortar shell, instantly shattering our timelessness and conjuring up serious decisions and planning. Mandy audibly gasped, and we looked at each other, sensing the other's apprehension, before turning away and ignoring the silent dilemma.

I felt rejuvenated, focused and happy but couldn't see how a return home, to a 'normal' life, was going to maintain this utopia. I didn't want to reignite a marriage where I was absent and we talked on remote control about domestic necessities. We'd become so in tune over the past ten months, reconnecting like we had in our courtship days. 'Home', the Australia home not the rolling Franki one, only represented a threat to this renewed existence.

The next morning I trudged into the Amex office and, at the point of giving up all hope, the papers arrived. I came whooping back into camp, waving at the peroxide blonde in reception and my friend the prostitute on the street outside. We were up at dawn and gone. Freedom never felt so good.

On the road, I did a date check and confirmed the World Cup started in a few days. We could still make it. Mandy was happy to take up this challenge, so we powered along a new, empty EU-sponsored motorway, getting as much space between us and Bulgaria as possible. We slashed across Serbia and then through Croatia and back into the EU sanctuary of Slovenia. After two days, one service station sleep, 1,000 kilometres, four countries and three eastern border crossings, we no longer needed to show our green card to anyone.

When we eventually pulled off the highway into Bled it was as though we had arrived inside a storybook setting. The campground fronted a perfect shimmering alpine lake which was backed by snow-capped mountains. A castle perched on one of the cliffs over the lake and a church sat on a small island in the middle. For the first time in weeks, we had hot showers. There were playgrounds and parks, free internet and a restaurant at the front door. No litter of homeless puppies pissed on our feet. No fat men wanted me to suck them off. We took the kids on train rides and walks around the lake and basked in the sun on the lawns. Every now and then I checked the green papers, treating them like winning lottery numbers that I had still yet to claim.

I looked at the calendar again and, although we still had more time left on this trip than most people spend on annual holidays, the end was in sight. Mandy had silently sensed my growing misgivings, linked as they were to her own. 'What if we keep going?' she ventured one night.

'What do you mean?' I knew exactly what she meant.

'You know, why stop at twelve months? We own the camper. We could just keep going... like the French family.'

'Hmmm... Hmmm,' I double murmured like a priest in a confessional. She'd enunciated my very thoughts, producing that same zing of excitement I'd experienced when we first planned the trip and then when we walked the plank and jumped off into Estonia and later Morocco. The thought of 'could we really' hit deep and was back again. It was an alluring concept – just keep on going. One life – live it.

We fell into a dangerous silence, leaving the idea to ferment, and I could tell by the mutual sparkle in our eyes that we might have just changed direction in life.

14

DARING TO DREAM

The kangaroo lay grim and quiet on the ground, reflecting the mood of the thousands of people standing in eerie silence around its plastic carcass. It was the eighty-third minute of Australia's first football World Cup match in thirty-two years, and they were losing.

We were sitting on a grassy hill at the fan-fest within Munich's Olympic stadium. I voiced my concerns to Mandy. 'If we don't beat Japan, we're stu—' Screams from the massive speakers drowned out my diagnosis. 'Timmy Caaar-heeeeeeeeeell!'

Plastic cups of beer flew upwards like a thousand erupting mini volcanoes, the blow-up kangaroos started hopping, the green and gold army went ballistic. Then Cahill snapped another one and minutes later, in extra time, John Aloisi scored a third to seal the win.

The Socceroos had never before scored a single World Cup goal, let alone three in seven minutes. They were the second lowest-ranked team in the tournament and had been the last to qualify. Their quest for football's holy grail had begun in earnest.

Jaimie was on my shoulders and Mandy was terrifying Callum by spinning him around to the tune of Men at Work's 'Down Under'. That third goal was the starting pistol for an outrageous weeks-long party that would tear us away from any homeward-bound distractions.

Four days earlier we had pulled into Munich's Thalkirchen campsite. It was set on the Isar River opposite the Hellabrunn zoo, surrounded by a forest and parks. We chose a site next to the children's playground, one of the few remaining as they were the least popular. The sandpit happened to be near the TV room, the café, supermarket and a beer-dispensing machine, so it was a perfect base for our entire family.

We occupied the days before the tournament exploring more wholesome activities than beer and football. We went to the zoo, rode the metro, ate bratwurst and sauerkraut and watched the dancing figurines in the town's clock tower. We regularly went to the nearby forest, which had a narrow fast-flowing alpine stream running through its grounds, which partygoers floated down to blast off dull heads.

Thalkirchen quickly swelled to capacity. Campers, motor homes, tour buses and backpackers were pouring in, all emblazoned with their national colours, and the site soon became an international party every day, starting well before the 3 p.m. kick-off of the early game and finishing in the wee hours. Rafts with noisy oompah bands cruised down the Isar. Satellite televisions were set up outside the modern motor homes, barbecues blazed and music blared. A flotilla of Brazilians brought their own brand of drums, whistles and dancing, as each night evolved into a nationalist war of classic Australian music competing with the relentless South American drumbeat.

The kids were constantly hijacked by other campers, running up to us covered with facepaint in the colours of other countries. I had to keep scrubbing English flags off their cheeks. For nights on end we struggled to get to sleep, mostly because we were outside dancing and partying while the kids slept inside.

Mechtild, a German friend of ours, visited the camp one day, but after a trip to the crammed, smelly toilets, she thought we needed saving from the chaos. 'Why don't you stay in my apartment?' she offered. 'I'll be away on holidays. It's a luxury penthouse with 200 metres of terraces.'

After months of frugal living, the thought of having a respite in separate bedrooms, luxuriating in a warm shower that didn't switch off after two minutes and washing clothes in something other than a bucket was an almost inconceivable fantasy, like Australia winning the World Cup. I knew also that Mandy, while tolerating my sporting fanaticism, would be keen to escape.

'Oh, look, thanks so much, but we'll have to knock your offer back.'

I wheeled around and stared at my wife.

'We're having too much fun here.' She waved around at the campsite.

'You'd prefer to stay *here*?' Mechtild asked. I rested back on my haunches, interested to see what alien life-force had taken possession of my wife. She wasn't just mildly disinterested in sport, she had once asked me if Greg Norman played rugby league.

'Well, yeah, but it's not about the football,' Mandy said. 'We're just having such a great time. The kids are playing with dozens of others. We're meeting loads of people. Johnny and I are having turns to go out. I'd love to stay in luxury, of course, but we'd miss out.'

We'd come a long way from our Norway days when we just wanted to hide from the world. Now we couldn't get enough of people. This decision to forgo material comfort was the first tangible thing we'd done that indicated that maybe we had broken away from our years of entrenched thinking.

The next day was my turn for a Big Day Out, so I wandered over to a neighbouring van and told the father that Mandy was taking the kids to the zoo for the day. 'Do you want to go to the fan-fest and watch England play?'

Rod was a family man, travelling Europe in a motor home with his kids as well, so it was unlikely he could go. 'I'll get my wallet,' was his reply.

Inside Munich's Olympic grounds, we jumped on a carousel that was actually a rotating bar. Once on, there was just one problem hampering my enjoyment. It was seven euros for a beer. 'Plus two more for a deposit for the bloody cup!' I exclaimed after returning from the bar. My weekly restaurant allowance would be drained by one cup of fluid. I soon realised, though, that the deposits were refundable, but no one seemed to know that. I grabbed some empty cups from a nearby table before the waiters could take them, strutted up to the bar and handed over ten empty cups and ordered two Weissbiers. The hulking German bartender took the empties, counted them, poured steins, wiped the froth flat with a stick, and slid the full ones back at me. I wheeled around to scamper away, but he dropped his giant hand on my shoulder and barked something in German. I turned slowly to accept my fate as he dropped six euro coins into my shirt pocket. The refund was more than the cost of the beers.

'*Danke,*' I gasped.

As the night and the cup collections progressed the great challenge was no longer money but stepping on and off the carousel to go to the toilet.

It felt like I was still on the carousel the next morning. Mandy couldn't understand the attraction in watching footy while sitting on carousel horses but I didn't have the strength to explain they had been replaced by tables and chairs.

I was keen to get tickets to a game, but they were all sold out. Rather than wallow, I spent days hyping Mandy and the kids up to our big day at the fan-fest: Australia versus Brazil, arguably the greatest and most popular football team on the planet. Win or lose, it would be one of the pinnacles of Australian sporting triumph.

In preparation, I had clad Franki in Australian flags and bought us all gold T-shirts which we wore every day. We set up posts in front of the van, and kicked goals every afternoon, running around aeroplane-style yelling 'Goooooaaaaall!' each time one snuck past Callum's unmoving hands. Jaimie was practising the words to 'Advance Australia Fair'. We were anticipating the event as the greatest family day out ever, and then Rod rushed in and destroyed it all. 'I can get two tickets for the Brazil game. Three hundred euros each. Scalpers are everywhere. Want one, Johnno?'

I gasped. This was like winning the lottery.

Mandy instantly said I should do it. 'You'll never get this chance again,' she said. 'You only live once. Remember the bears!'

There was no hesitation in my reply. I turned to Rod happily and said, 'No thanks, mate, not this time.'

'What?' he cried, gasping for air like a goldfish out of its tank.

'What?' Mandy cried, gasping like the goldfish's mother.

'I can't,' I said. 'I can't. Look at the kids. They're so excited about this.'

'They'll get over it,' Mandy said.

'Yeah I know, but I *want* to watch it with them.' We'd been having too much fun together as a family, this week, these past months. I had promised this great day out and this was one promise I had no intention, or desire, of breaking. I could almost hear my sports-frenzied mates' voices. They'd accuse me of all sorts of politically incorrect biases and sexual desires for an array of animals, wrapping up with, 'You've changed, man'. And they would have been right.

With Brazil playing, the fan-fest was packed. We sang our lungs out to the national anthem, the first time I had done that with the kids. The sparkle in their eyes was better than any ticket.

Brazil won 2–0, an unexpectedly close game that started a buzz that maybe the Socceroos could achieve more than anyone thought possible.

We decided to continue the party and follow the Australian team to Stuttgart for their next game against Croatia. But on arrival we found the city's campground had overflowed to a bitumen car park. The area was enclosed with temporary metal fencing allowing rows of vans to wedge in and share temporary toilet facilities. It didn't matter.

The night of the game, I watched as my non-sporty, book-reading partner dressed the kids in gold and rallied people in the campsite to commandeer a neighbouring motor home's TV.

With minutes left in the game, Australia was about to exit the tournament when Harry Kewell scored and drew the game 2–2. Suddenly the throngs of fans were now plotting the unimaginable: Australia beating Italy in the quarter final.

After the game I listened to Mandy brief our fellow campers. 'Right,' she said, 'we will be in Kaiserslautern for the Italy game. Kennedy and Kewell might be injured and we have some yellow cards against us. We've a chance if Viduka's fit and we can't rule out the Goose factor.'

'Goose, goose, goose!' everyone chanted as was now tradition whenever coach Guus Hiddink's name was mentioned.

She continued, 'But we have to watch out as Italy is good at dives and creating fouls.'

I was astonished. Until now, Mandy had thought Kewell was a climate zone, a dive was under water and a foul was a chicken. The transition was complete. Sporting aliens had finally taken total possession of her.

We woke the next morning feeling as though our social power pack was thoroughly drained. The past ten days had been as though we'd been in some bizarre state of centrifugal motion, spinning from one constant party to another. We needed a break.

The city of Freiburg was peacefully set deep in the Black Forest; a glorious choice to counterbalance the footballing hedonism. For lunch we treated ourselves to a Chinese meal. The table was round and contained a rotating lazy Susan, ideal for conversation and for small teddy bears to ride on. Once the obligatory fried rice was ordered, it occurred to me that we hadn't been together, just the four of us, for nearly two weeks. While we had been collectively socialising between playgrounds, fan-fests and campground dinners, our connectivity with the kids had become lost in the noise.

This was how we had lived in our pre-Franki frenetic world. Always busy, kiddy-time often unfocused and elsewhere, on the phone at the playground or working at home and fooling ourselves that being on premises meant being 'there'. My kids just wanted Mandy and me to look them in the eye and listen, talk and play.

We wanted that now too. Fortunately this current sense of disconnect didn't feel irretrievable like it did after London. A few days of hanging together would have us back calling carrots by name and inviting toys to dinner. But I realised that this challenge would never go away. There would always be some great event, invite, electronic device or work calling. Whether we stayed on the road or returned home, we would have to ring-fence our family times, at dinner, going on holidays, or just going to the beach. Inviting nobody else, clearing head space and turning those phones off, disconnecting to remain truly connected.

These thoughts and the peace of the day, however, were broken that evening.

'We just got tickets to the Italy game!' an Aussie chap travelling with his wife and four kids beamed at me.

He explained how Football Australia had announced extra tickets for any Australians who were in Stuttgart as long as they showed up with their passports.

'I guess there were only a few?' I asked, willing this to be true.

'Oh shit no! Everyone who was there got some.'

I turned, walked to the van and crawled under my bedcovers.

I later regrouped and rang the hotel where the tickets were and was told there were some left if we got there early in the morning. By 8.20 p.m. we were on the road back to Stuttgart. The 'four of us' time would have to wait.

The city was in party meltdown when we arrived near midnight. England was playing the next day and the flag of St George was flapping everywhere. People were dancing around the streets and blowing horns. 'Drive to the Football Australia hotel,' I instructed Mandy. I wanted us in pole position for the tickets.

'But parking will be impossible,' she rightly pointed out.

'No worries. I have a plan.'

She groaned.

We pulled into the circular driveway of the plush five-star hotel. Two red-coated concierges, who looked like they should have been guarding Buckingham Palace, watched as I popped out of the side door, having shaved and changed into long pants, a collared shirt and shiny black shoes, clothes that had been unused for the entire trip.

I strolled through the brass revolving doors, across the marbled foyer and up to reception as though I owned the hotel. '*Guten tag*,' I smiled. 'I have a meeting with the Football Federation of Australia tomorrow.' When she saw our dirty beast shadowing their beautiful foyer, she tried valiantly to hide her five-star grimace. 'Would it be possible to park here tonight for my meeting?'

Surprisingly, this worked and I was marshalled outside to the concierge who opened the gates to the security parking.

Successful as my charade had been, the next day there were no tickets left.

'Well, you didn't die wondering.' Mandy tried to brighten my mood. 'And we saved twenty euros on camping fees!'

'No worries, I've got another plan,' I declared.

If the Socceroos could dare to achieve the impossible, so could I.

'What next?' Mandy exhaled.

The morning of the Italy game, I went to Kaiserslautern's train station, theorising that train stations were always a hotbed of corruption. Mandy had insisted that if successful, I just get two tickets and go with Mick, our friend from Attila's in Turkey who was now in Germany, as she would rather spend the money on something else. I soon spotted a respectable-looking grey-haired gentleman among a huddle of young fans. I glided up behind them and listened as the lads refused to pay 160 euros for a ticket. I stepped in and bought two.

The city had turned into a festival and one of the town's squares had been converted into a virtual Aussie headquarters.

Mick and I followed the music and instantly hit a barrage of green and gold and plastic kangaroos. Over the next hour, the music and songs blurred together as the place rocked out with Aussie classics. We sang away with the best of them.

The ditty 'Tie Me Kangaroo Down, Sport' came blaring out and everyone was jigging and pretending to flap wobble boards (this was before the allegations against the song's singer Rolf Harris surfaced, and hence the tune was still popular). Then the song moved into a fourth verse where the dying farmer screeched derogatorily about 'Abos', and his wish to let them out of captivity, as they were of no further use to him.

All movement and singing stopped. 'What the fuck was that?' the bloke next to me blurted.

Astonished, confused and angry faces glared around. The Germans in the crowd were completely perplexed. The whole tournament had been featuring a 'Say No to Racism' campaign and here was an Australian tune, booming out on our country's finest sporting day, full of racism.

I would later find out that the verse was removed in 1960. I, like most of the crowd, had never heard or even known about this dreaded 'fourth verse'.

The crowd's frozen reaction was spontaneous as a collective shame seemed to settle over us.

Slowly but eventually, the square pulsated back to life courtesy of Mental as Anything's 'Live it Up', but that mass reaction made me prouder of my kinsmen than any sporting achievement. I figured that if this football-hungry mob was representative of the intolerance today's generation has for racism, then we must be heading in the right direction.

Ninety game-time minutes had passed and Australia had pulled off the miracle. Mick and I were high up in the stands, it was 0–0 and the Azzurri were down to ten men. Extra time would almost certainly deliver an Aussie victory and the carnival would be on the road to Berlin.

What I thought would be a temporary diversion to a fun tournament, an escape from reality before having to face reality, had become a master class in witnessing a group of men's progression against the odds. They seemed to have no fear of failure, just an innate giant-killing aspiration that anything was possible. It was almost too much to believe. Italy were the second most successful team in the history of the World Cup. They had played a form of the game since medieval times and had won more championships than any other nation. Could we dare to dream that the upstart Aussies could brazenly storm the pantheon of history?

Then the whistle screeched a penalty and every shade of blue in the stadium launched into the air. A player was down inside the Australian penalty box with seconds to go in the game.

'It's a dive! A dive!' screamed Mick.

Fabio Grosso's acrobatic tumble would be debated for years as to whether it was a fake dive. But that didn't help right now. The next few minutes were a blur as I stared down at the goals, willing with every brain particle for the kick to miss.

The Italian fans were roaring, stamping and shaking the stadium so hard I thought it might collapse. And then the ball, in slow motion, floated into the net.

It was a horrible way for the dream to end. I had become so inculcated into believing the impossible that it hurt with surprise physicality.

We eventually escaped the stadium and joined a rather sombre lot of supporters back in the town centre. As we walked, Italians roared past with flags, sometimes stopping to shake hands, shrugging as if to say, shit happens.

The local Germans were just as gutted but kept shaking our hands as though we had played in the game. 'Your country has achieved great things. You must be very proud.'

And we were. The team had tried everything to break with convention and, in chasing their holy grail, battling the wins and losses, they achieved more than they ever dared.

I hoped the same would be true for us.

15

THE FRENCH CONNECTION

Six weeks was longer than most people would have for annual holidays in their life and yet this remaining time on our journey seemed terrifyingly short. Since leaving Kaiserslautern, we'd done a good job of ignoring our imminent departure. At first we were aimless, just following the Rhine River, debilitated and let-down, not from the football loss, but from readjusting to the social vacuum of just the four of us. We never wanted the party to end, and yet, soon it would. The real world, with its snare of responsibility, lay waiting to pounce like a lion in the grass.

Mandy and I were determined that these six weeks would not be filled with concerns about jobs and money and future tasks. Instead, we pulled out a map and started plotting where we might travel to, weighing up a plethora of options that would titillate any visitor to Europe – Switzerland, Austria, Germany, Prague. But the overriding decision had to be confronted. Should we stay beyond the year or should we go? It sounded very much like a Clash song, which indicated that if we went, there would be trouble, if we stayed there would be more trouble, so this thought process wasn't helping at all.

Fortunately we no longer hid from these decisions like we so desperately did when traversing Scandinavia in what seemed like a lifetime ago. This year out had steeled us with the resilience to confront life's challenges head on without delay, to be brave. And so, with the seriousness of scientists puzzling over the solution to world hunger, Mandy and I sat staring at the sky in intense thoughtful silence. Finally, after what seemed like an age, I leapt up. 'I've got it!'

'Yes! What? What's the answer?'

'Let's go to Paris!'

Mandy jumped on this suggestion as well.

The Paris campground was perched on the banks of the Seine River in the Bois de Boulogne, a massive 8,500-square-kilometre park that was a remnant of the ancient forest of Rouvray that once spread unbroken to Normandy.

An English couple were ahead of us at check-in, angrily accusing the Parisian hosts of deliberately not understanding their requests for a nice campsite. We stood behind in amused silence. The French, of course, were notorious for not trying too hard when others don't, and eventually the English tourists stormed out spitting, 'Rude French pigs!'

'*Cochon,*' I whispered to Mandy.

'What?'

'*Cochon*. French word for pig.' I then smiled at the receptionist and said, '*Bonjour!*'

One local word, mangled or mismanaged, but attempted, was the simplest of travellers' keys to opening up a world of hospitality, even in France. Our check-in went nicely and we were given a prime spot on the river. The English couple were next to the toilets.

The Bois de Boulogne was a chaotic mixture of impeccably groomed gardens, hidden buildings, sparkling fountains and dishevelled forest. Almost every book I had read that was set in Paris seemed to have a grisly murder in the Bois de Boulogne, so it was clearly an ideal place to take children. We wandered through it the next day, finding quiet little pockets in which to sit and think. I had also read that in 1060 William the Conqueror sat in a quiet spot here, possibly right where I was, and had an epiphany to fight for the throne of England.

I was hoping my own visit might also inspire some great vision as to whether we should conquer returning home or not. I could then be John the Returner.

When we went into central Paris, we were in the eye of the high season tourist storm. It was belting hot at thirty-nine degrees and the crowds were thick and jostling. We waited two hours in line for the Eiffel Tower, another hour to change lifts halfway, had three glorious minutes at the top, and an exhausting scramble back down. By the end, Callum had morphed into a sobbing mess. It was not the Eiffel experience of my dreams, but the kids regained their sparkle by running through water sprinklers at the base of the tower in the Champ de Mars.

Partially revitalised, we set off in search of the ultimate traditional Parisian lunch. I envisaged a café where my friendly one local word 'Bonjour' would be reciprocated with a favoured terrace seat among bright flowers and wall art. Violins would be playing. We would be served an array of French specialties – onion soup, mussels in white wine, beef bourguignon, baskets of bread, all washed down with a spectacular carafe of Bordeaux.

But the heat had drained the kids' personalities away, and it was soon clear that a long decadent lunch with them flopping around on the floor like beached catfish would be about as enjoyable as sticking forks into our eyes. There was only one go-to option. We pulled the restaurant emergency lever. 'Two kids' packs *et deux* Big Mac meals... *s'il vous plait.*' Chez Macca was, after all, air conditioned, cheap and had a stream of soft-serve ice cream that could temporarily slay the demons within any child.

In 1999, French farmers had led a nationwide revolt to stop the global hamburger chain arriving. Their leader even claimed that using French cheese in these establishments was akin to sex shops selling holy water.

He couldn't stop the invasion, and for now, I was glad, but still, as I slurped on my watery Coke, I looked wistfully towards the true French café across the road. 'You know,' I said to Mandy, 'sometimes travelling with kids is like being behind bars in a prison cell with the keys to freedom just out of reach.'

Jaimie had a different perspective. 'This is the best lunch ever, Daddy!'

At least someone was having their dream Parisian cuisine.

Summer in Europe meant late sundown, so we woke the kids at 11 p.m. because I insisted on salvaging something from our Paris visit and seeing the Eiffel Tower's light show. We drove in and parked on the banks of the Seine, enjoying the glittering display, until an irate traffic officer thumped on our window and pointed to a sign that had a Ghostbusters slash through an image of a parked motor home. We drove off quickly, now seeing these signs everywhere around central Paris. This was understandable. At fifty-five euros per night in camp fees, campers would nest all over the city like they did in Spain and Portugal if they could.

With nowhere to park, the visit reverted to a drive, breaking one of our ensconced rules, cemented after the Warsaw and Casablanca driving debacles, of never deliberately ploughing our machine into the thick of city traffic. We rumbled the big Franki beast around the city and slowly up the Champs-Élysées, cruising parallel to open-top convertibles and past the glitterati of the world's greatest shops. Each of us cried out when we saw an impressive globally recognisable icon.

'Notre-Dame!' I yelled.

'The Louvre!' Mandy pointed.

'McDonald's!' Jaimie and Callum screeched.

At the top of the Champs-Élysées, we charged on into the heaving lanes of traffic whirring around the Arc de Triomphe. Even at midnight, it was busy, and it immediately felt as though we had entered a dodgem car arena.

'Go round, just once,' I said to Mandy.

We completed one slow terrifying lap as vehicles busily charged onto the roundabout from the twelve avenues that fed into it, blasting their horns and acknowledging our clumsy presence with single-finger salutes. The road rules were a muddle of confusion. No one knew who to give way to. It was clear the only logical thing to do was to get out of this maelstrom of madness.

But Jaimie had other ideas, yelling from the back, 'Go round again, Mummy!'

Mandy and I looked at each other and shrugged in a typical French way. We went round and round the Arc de Triomphe five more times, singing, calling out and laughing all the way. We figured the lumbering Franki was big, old and clearly driven by idiots, and consequently other drivers would be well advised to give us some space. They did just that.

With our budget being blasted by the daily camp fees and each transit into Paris in sweltering heat becoming a hardship, we resolved to do 'Paris for adults' another time, on another budget.

And so we left Paris, symbolically driving further away from our departure airport in Amsterdam, cruising west through the Loire Valley. The driving view along the Loire River to Blois was filled with a sea of bright yellow sunflowers and glimpses of some of the 300 châteaux built in the region. The valley was once the holiday home of kings and their hangers-on. We decided to visit at least one château, so with an awful lot of cultural discussion, picked the biggest one: the Château de Chambord had 440 rooms and stables for 1,200 horses.

I felt somewhat humbled on our return to our castle on wheels. The real castle had been dark and cool, but our fort was hot, very hot. Fortunately there was a public pool adjacent to the campground. Mandy had a cold so decided to take the kids and just watch over them. I had six pages left in a book, so agreed to follow along shortly.

When I arrived later, Mandy was being frog-marched out of the pool area by two uniformed attendants. 'My kids!' she was yelling. '*Les enfants!* They are in the *piscine*. They can't swim!'

I rushed over. 'What did you do?' I called above the kerfuffle.

'I don't bloody know! They were yabbering at me and I couldn't understand them and they got really mad and dragged me out!'

I could see the children inside in the wading pool with two other tots and their mother. The woman waved at me, establishing she was watching them.

The argument continued. Mandy was attempting to explain that the kids couldn't swim and had been left unattended, but she was physically blocked each time she tried to re-enter the pool area.

With my school French, I slowly deciphered their message. 'They're saying you're not allowed near the pool without swimmers,' I said.

'So what? I'm not fucking swimming!' The attendants seemed unaware that getting in the way of a protective mother was like standing in front of flowing molten lava.

Finally, the chief pool attendant arrived. 'It is France hygiene laws,' he explained in broken English. 'You can't wear anything in the pool area that can be worn outside.'

He handed me a brief information sheet that detailed that street clothes can have items in their pockets, and fibres and chemicals on them, which can clog and upset pool systems. Bacteria and E. coli were the two big dangers.

'Oh I get it.' I laughed in Mandy's direction, 'You are an airborne threat.'

This attempt at levity was not appreciated by my fuming wife. What was funny was that Australia had more pools per capita, and I had never heard of this. But we were literally on the wrong side of the fence to debate the wisdom of leaving small children unattended in a pool as a preference to clogging the pool filter. I figured that while French rules could be somewhat confusing to the outsider, it was best to work with them, not against them. After all, this was a country in which it was a law that UFOs could not be flown over vineyards in the Rhône region and that you can't name a pig Napoleon.

'I go in and get *les enfants*,' I said in my best Hercule Poirot accent, confident my use of French words would crack the solution.

The officious attendant scanned my Billabong surf shorts. '*Non, monsieur.* You cannot. You must wear swimmers.'

'These are swimmers.'

He shook his head negative.

'But I only ever wear them swimming.'

'But you are wearing them now, *monsieur*.'

He had me. 'Well, how do you suggest I get my kids?'

'No problem. You can borrow a pair of swimmers.' He held up a box of used Lycra Speedos.

I looked at him in horror.

For health and safety reasons I had to put on someone else's Speedos. But Mandy had now found a moment of joy in the situation and reached in and handed me a bright red pair. 'These'll look good on you,' she said.

I held up what looked like a thong, not knowing which was worse – letting the kids drown or wearing Speedos in public.

But I had no choice. I took the compulsory shower and faked nonchalance, strolling across the pool past a dozen fit, tanned frolicking bodies. Fortunately, no one paid any attention to my glistening white torso and the ring marks where my limbs turned brown from a lifetime of wearing surf attire. I reached the kids successfully, relieved at not having drawn any overt attention.

'Daddeee!' Jaimie screamed in surprise. 'What are you wearing?'

Callum looked up at my scantily clad two-tone body and gave out a high-pitched squeal louder than any peacock.

Everyone in the pool area turned and stared at me.

Still on the move, we headed further west to the Bay of Biscay, then up through Brittany and across to St Malo where we met up with Chrissie, boyfriend Martin and his daughter Meg, who had flown in for another catch-up. Chris and Martin had a tent and Meg would sleep in our camper.

We camped on the ocean front and filled our days wandering the throbbing lanes inside St Malo's walled old town from the 1400s; strolling over its ramparts; eating cured ham, cheese and tubs of garlic mussels; swimming in the freezing waters and hovering over the kids in case the six-metre tides turned and came in fast.

It would be this hovering, or lack of, that would lead to our decision. One morning, Mandy disappeared off with Chris. Martin and Meg went wandering, and I was left with the little people. I had come to love my time alone with the kids. It was such a contrast to the scant attention I had dispensed in my previous 'throw the dog a bone' parenting years.

I took them to the beach and let them run off onto the vast sands which were exposed for miles at low tide. I periodically looked up from my book to watch them splash gleefully in shallow pools of water. On one occasion, I noticed a woman approach the kids, attempt to talk to them and then pivot her head around. She was obviously looking for their guardian and I was sitting well beyond her acceptable hover zone.

After witnessing the power of the pool filter laws, I didn't want to be reported to the French equivalent of Child Services, and so I dragged myself off the towel and across the flats. The woman blasted me with a verbal spray, but the benefit of not understanding the language was that I couldn't be insulted.

I knew that she meant well, but if she wanted to treat kids like dogs on a short leash that was her issue. I just wanted to give them some taste of freedom and adventure. It wasn't as though they were rollerblading through Kabul, but overriding fear seems to have swamped children's freedom.

I didn't want to become a 'what-ifer', doing nothing and risking nothing, and then developing kids that do nothing and risk nothing.

As I looked around the beach at other children with their barnacle mums attached, I realised that I had to keep my kids away from the suffocating lifestyle that was becoming the global norm. And then the solution rushed in on me like the tide. The answer I had hoped to find in the Bois de Boulogne had washed up on the shores of the Côtes-d'Armor and I was struck dumb by its simplicity. We were living this lifestyle right now. We had been free of this type of judgement, both as parents, and as people, for a year. It had proven to be invigorating, soul-enriching, and free. Returning home would be a folly of re-entry back into the regulated world. With a gasp of enlightenment, my decision to stay was made.

Mandy later found us on the beach, with the kids happily building sandcastles next to me, a scene of well-tethered bliss. 'How's it going?' she asked.

'Oh great. I've been watching them like a hawk.'

'No, he hasn't,' Jaimie cried. 'We were playing out there,' she pointed off to where the tide had now rushed in. 'And Daddy stayed here until a lady got mad at him and told him to look after us.'

I later told Mandy about the attack by the 'what-ifer' and all the world's regulations I wanted to avoid. I hadn't detailed my yearning to keep travelling but Jaimie seemed to have a sixth sense and shuffled over to us. 'Are we going home to Australia soon, Daddy?'

She was clearly hopeful of an affirmative and there had obviously been some bunk-bed propaganda going on, as Callum stood next to her waiting for my answer. 'Are we going to drive there in Franki?' he asked.

'Well, you know what? When we do go home,' I said to the children, 'we have to spend a lot more time with Nana and everyone else we know. Nana turns eighty this year!'

We had been writing so many letters to her that Nana had become an almost extended member of this trip. 'Will she let us play with the toy cars and give us jelly beans?' was the next high priority question, followed by other great ambitions. Will we have our own rooms? How many teddies can we have? Does our house still have a pool? Can we start school? And finally Jaimie asked, 'Are we going to her party?'

This final question pulled me up like a handbrake.

'Well, I don't know,' I answered slowly, 'we might not be home by then.'

The kids' hopeful gaze was like a glorious shaft of light breaking through heavy clouds, suddenly illuminating future possibilities where all I had seen was hometown drudgery. I looked at them for a minute and realised they saw the return home as just another fabulous stage in their adventure, one that would include friends, school, toy cars and jelly beans. They had no problem juggling rules that sometimes seemed confusing and mixing everyday life with fun, side by side.

In contrast, I had been focusing on all the negatives – the challenges, the money, the resettling, and the overwhelming belief that everything we had embraced on the road would dissipate on touchdown. And that by not being out seeing deserts, mountains and castles every other day, Australia would represent a deadening return to the treadmill. But it didn't have to be that way.

The next morning dawned bright and sunny. I woke in our top bunk and pulled down the blind to peek out across the English Channel. I didn't know what Mandy had taken from the discussion with the kids, but as she stirred, I decided to moot my backflip to her.

'I'm thinking I'm ready,' I whispered in the dawn light.

'Oh no, we can't!' Mandy vehemently whispered back.

'Why not?'

'Why not?' she whispered at me astounded. 'Because Meg's asleep on the kitchen table below us.'

'Not sex!' I whispered, although the idea wasn't the worst I'd ever heard. 'I'm talking about going home. I'm ready.'

Her instant stillness was creepy. 'Oh my god,' she eventually gasped. 'Chrissie and I discussed that for hours last night.'

'Yeah,' I drawled, 'and what did you two decide?'

Her next words were going to be critical. 'I'm ready too,' she said.

'You're kidding? What about travel?'

'Oh, travel-smazel. It'll still be there. There's so much we have to do!'

She then outlined the excitement she had about returning to Australia, the chance for her to start writing again, and getting the kids settled at school and making friends. In return, I pulled out my diary and scanned the weird list of ideas I had scratched down as we had travelled. Business ideas, volunteer work, simpler living, moving to the beach, and concepts like kids' barber shops with mini motorcycle seats, or baguette makers as home appliances. Some were just ridiculous and others dared me to wheel off in a completely different direction and indulge in things I had always wanted to, things that no one would ever associate with me. Maybe I could write? Become a greenie? The ideas were zinging. Going home started to represent an outrageous opportunity to change everything and embark on an altered life with new purpose and fun. It would mean walking the plank again and jumping further than we ever had before.

With renewed freshness, we kissed our trio of friends goodbye and headed to Chartres where we met up with Esther and Rodney for a final few rounds of triple-strength gin and tonics. They had been cruising slowly around Europe on their own jaunt for the past six months. They'd decided to stay as long as possible and had detoured hundreds of kilometres to see us off. The heatwave continued and we spent the next four days hiding in the shade of the trees and emptying the camper of our few worldly possessions.

It was a long, sad goodbye to Franki. I recalled the first sight of the motor home, dusty, decrepit, on life support with cables to its bonnet. I had thought then that I had made one of the biggest mistakes of my life, and the following weeks delivered very little that opposed that view. Her claustrophobic size had been one of the key triggers that had tested us. Our flaws as parents, partners and people had been exposed. But over time she had become the magic transporter that helped us rediscover our *joie de vivre*. She rated, quite simply, as the greatest home we had ever had.

We finally drove north to Amsterdam, leaving Rodney and Esther behind to continue their own quest.

And then it was all over, as sudden as a passing thunderstorm. We treated Franki like a car again, handed the papers, including the very fresh green card, over to Donna for resale, and walked away.

Two days later we were sitting on the floor in Amsterdam's Schiphol airport. The kids were drawing in their puzzle books. Mandy was buying food with the last of our euros.

I was people-watching. A family was huddled around their teenage daughter who was sobbing and hugging her mother, setting off on her first solo voyage. The little brother was holding her daypack. The father was standing aloof with tears in his eyes.

Around us, lovers embraced, breaking up or reuniting. Groups were going off to weddings, grief was etched on faces going to funerals, newborns were being introduced to grandparents, North Sea workers were arriving home to their wives and babies, people held balloons and waited, emitting screams of delight or sobbing with tears. The airport contained people expressing their feelings in ways they wouldn't have in their normal daily lives. For just a few moments, they were shedding their skins and exposing themselves. I smiled. We had learnt to do just that over the past twelve months in Franki.

Then I spotted a familiar, recognisable figure. A suited caricature weaved through the crowd and out to the taxi stand. His eyes were fixed, his face was blank. He towed a black luggage trolley behind and his cell phone was wedged firmly in his ear.

The former me.

This sight unsettled me at surprising speed. What would I do for work? How would we steer the kids through school and still live the alternate life I had been so committed to only days before? Look at that man with the briefcase. What an easy path. The only clear, definable path. Take the shortcut back into working suburbia. It paid the bills. My career would soar again. And it made me want to stick my head in a bucket of sewer water.

This easy shortcut would just take me back to where I started. That would mean backtracking. And I would do anything to avoid that.

Our plane was called. As we walked through the gates I slowly scanned across the word 'Departures'.

'Departure to where?' I thought. 'To what?'

There was a backlit advertisement behind the gates asking if we knew where we were going.

I tapped Mandy on the shoulder and pointed at it. We laughed a little nervously, shrugged and held the kids' hands tight. I knew only one thing. We were still on the road... with kids.

Epilogue

RETURN TO THE CIRCUS

Within metres of entering the first major shopping centre I'd been in for a year, I was surrounded by bright flashing neon and advertisements promising to fulfil my every desire. Bouncy jingles were guaranteeing to deliver a life of happiness through no deposit, no interest offers. It was all at amazing never-to-be-repeated discounts and the waft from the food court smelt irresistible.

I charged back out onto the street, sucking in air and muttering like a mad hobo, 'We never should have returned, never, ever, ever!' People walked around me in a wide circle, clearing my path as I bustled home to tell everyone not to go out.

But when I got home no one was there. I stood at the doorway before slowly walking into the silence. The living room was stacked with unpacked boxes and a note lay pinned on the top of one. It read, 'Johnny, telephone connected. Internet on in a week. Gone to enrol Jaimie in pre-school, Callum at kindy, sign attached forms. See bills. Aaargh! Let's go back. Will get KFC. Love me, xxoo.'

Bills were stacked next to the note. A doctor's letter confirmed an appointment for Mandy. The job section of the paper lay open, howling at me to slap on a tie and go to work in a tall building with other busy bees making money for the man, just like I always had.

I lay starfish on the floor, staring at the ceiling, contemplating the most vital issue – how many pieces of KFC would Mandy bring home?

Soon the mad painter's voice returned. 'Get out while you can! You'll be living between the lines before you know it!'

It was exactly as the pilgrims on the road to Santiago de Compostela had foretold. I was looking at familiar things through new eyes.

We'd been at a barbecue a day earlier where everyone talked about the same topics they'd talked about a year ago. On the way there, I'd run into a friend who asked where I'd been for the past few weeks. The world had turned on its axis 400 times since I last lay on this floor, but nothing had changed. I elbowed up and looked around. The size of our house seemed obscene after a year cosying up in a motor home. What the hell did we need all this space for? I didn't even want to live here anymore. This was the ultimate irony. Ever since I left university, I had been driven by the idea of living in the prestigious suburb with city views. I would have made it then! Over the years we had bought in cheap areas, then a suburb nearby, then our current house on the 'wrong' side of the hill. I was edging closer, positioned perfectly at base camp for the final climb. And now, finally, within distance of the summit, I saw the peak for what it was – a false deity.

As I lay there pondering this, the telephone rang. Our friend Michelle was getting married in North Queensland in two weeks. 'We've booked out a nudist resort for the wedding!'

'You want us to go nuddy with your relatives?' I instantly had snapshots of grannies, aunts and uncles all jostling freestyle at the fruit cake stand.

'No idiot. We booked the whole place. No one is going to be nude.'

That clarified, I replied, 'Sorry, can't come. No money. Gotta get a job.'

Another call came moments later. I felt very busy. My mate Mick burst down the line, 'What are you doing in two weeks' time?'

'Dunno.' My stock reply to keep options open depending on the offer.

'My brother's running a reggae festival in Cairns. Wanna come?'

'Oh wow. But, no, can't,' I repeated. 'Gotta get a job.'

I hung up and reverted to the starfish position, now feeling crushed into the floor. My mind drifted back to the days with Baptiste and Ulysses, when we rediscovered the zest for remaining forever young of mind, promising acts of spontaneity and total abandon. It was so much easier to be full of bravado when perched in a foreign country without a pile of domestic bills tearing at our freedom. My ultimate fear was coming true. We had returned to the circus and were about to take the same seats, with nothing changed but a better photo album.

I went outside, desperate to think, pacing the front yard like a lion at the zoo. By the time my travelling team returned, an idea had blossomed and I presented it succinctly by holding out my arms and screaming, 'Rooooaaaad trip!'

The reggae festival was a hoot and everyone wore clothes at the wedding, which was generally a relief. But of greater importance was that Mandy and I had done something outrageous... in our home country.

Weeks later we turned for home again. 'Let's go the inland route through Charters Towers,' I suggested.

'No backtracking?' Mandy replied.

'Exactly,' and this time we both knew I wasn't talking about the road trip.

But we no longer had the luxury of endless time. As much as it pained me to admit it out loud to my wife, we needed a plan, and we needed one fast.

So like surgeons turning the knife upon ourselves, we embarked on a personal autopsy on our slow driving days through central Queensland. We tapped into the learning, fears and revelations of our year out. We recognised that we had met so many 'elders' on the road whose most common and repeated regret was that they'd worked exhausting hours through their children's youth and later, when they had the bounty of the time this work produced, their kids were gone. If they could reverse time and change one thing, that would be it. And so 'the four of us' was easily identified as our central mantra – everything else would have to be moulded to fit around it.

We then started to paint a picture of our dream lifestyle. We knew we wanted to get off the treadmill and work at things that really lit our fire. Mandy desperately wanted to restart writing. But we didn't talk in terms of careers or income, instead focusing on how to live daily, and what we would have to do to achieve that.

Visions, goals and strategies were laid out, very corporate ideals for people trying to run hard from that. We identified that we wanted community living, a bit of old-fashioned 'How ya going?' over the fence post. We wanted the kids to minimise time in the electronic vortex and run free, climb trees, preferably near the beach and a fabulous coffee shop. We would conjure careers, earn less money, live more simply and be more sustainable. By the end of four driving days, the list of things that needed seismic change scared the shit out of us, a sure sign we were on the right path.

We returned recharged, ready for this new adventure, but then, in what seemed like an instant, we were smashed by one of life's tsunamis.

A specialist found a large lump in Mandy's liver. She needed surgery. Suddenly everything evaporated. Careers, hobbies, aspirations, it was all folly if she were gone.

The day before the operation, Mandy lay in the hospital. Words like 'cancer' and 'death' fluttered silent and thick in the air around us. I couldn't help but replay in my mind my own ranting from when I first convinced her to travel. 'Life can be snatched away in a nanosecond you know! Why does it have to take a massive tragedy in people's lives before they stop and think, shit, am I really enjoying this?'

We were holding hands and she smiled up at me, almost cannily linked to the same thought process. 'I'm so glad we've just had the last twelve months we had,' she said. 'At least if I died tomorrow, I can say I went out blazing... living and loving life to the max!'

For some strange reason we were both happy about that, figuring that if the reaper knocks, we could at least say, 'Up yours, mate! You didn't catch me out!'

A week later, the doctor declared the lump benign. 'We cut it out and the liver will regenerate,' he advised in a monotone that could never have signified the reprieve we felt.

That zapped lump was the final tipping point, reinforcing our commitment to change, and to do it fast before we talked ourselves out of it or had the chance washed away by some unforeseen circumstance.

We walked the plank and jumped, feeling the zing of the unknown all over again. We sold the big house with the eight air conditioners, moved to Australia's southern Gold Coast and started building an eco home in a small community in a pretty green valley near the beach. We set up home-based consultancies and structured our time so we could intertwine our life with Jaimie and Callum. We slashed expenses so we could earn less and retain our power of choice in work and play. Sometimes I wanted to scream and go back to a job where I would get paid more and people would think I was important because I had a great title. But mostly not.

But tsunamis come in waves and another rolled in soon after. My sister Maree rang and I could hardly compute what she was saying. Nance, my mum, had at best twelve months to live. Cancer again.

Throughout the following year, Mandy held the family and income together while I spent hours, days and months with Nance, watching silly movies with her and gossiping about *Days of Our Lives*, like we did when I was a kid and Dr Neil Curtis was still a doctor. Had we been trapped by our previous financial commitments, I wouldn't have had the freedom to spend that year with her. That choice would always be one of the great gifts from our year in Franki.

Nance wrote a note to us kids before she passed away. I found it in a drawer afterwards. It was filled with jokes and one-liners, and I could picture her chuckling away while writing it. Then she slipped in one last line. At eighty-one years of age, she wrote: 'Enjoy life. For it goes very quickly.'

Who would have thought? Eighty-one years, a pretty good dig on most measurements, and yet it still goes in a flash.

If we needed any more messages pounded at us, this was the final one.

Mandy started growing things in a garden where previously she had the uncanny ability to kill off the hardiest of flora. I started annoying my friends with the fervour of a newborn sustainability zealot. As proof of my intent, I bought a little blue car that drove on the whiff of petrol and made me feel like I should be singing Aqua's 'Barbie Girl' with Jaimie whenever I went out in it.

Mandy and I were both arm-wrestling with our former identities, and at times it felt as though I was shedding a skin. I'd spent my entire working life climbing the mountain and now the handbrake was loosened and I was sliding down the mountain with abandon.

There was a fairly general consensus among my peers that I had lost the plot. Try telling anyone in the logical world that you are writing a book and watch their eyes glaze over with sorrow for how far you have fallen. Tell them you don't expect to make money out of all the effort and they will be certain you are downright loco. Mister mum, tree-hugger, all sorts of jokey labels were fired in my direction, but I embraced these as a sign I was on the right path and deflected them with the efficiency of Wonder Woman.

One night during our weekly exploratory telephone conversations, I was waffling away to a friend, Brendan, about various schemes Mandy and I were plotting.

I told him that sometimes we were winning in these quests. Sometimes not. But on every occasion since our year out, whenever the four of us drove past a motor home, we would all point and scream 'Franki!' and remember that for us, for anyone, there was always the chance of a new way forward.

He eventually lost patience with my babbling. After all, he had not had the benefit of my 400-odd days of dangerous thinking. 'What are you guys doing, man?' he blurted. 'You're just trying to live at home as if you are still on the road.'

I smiled yet another secret smile. Finally, someone else got it.

Appendix

HOW MUCH DID IT COST?

This question keeps popping up. I must have subconsciously anticipated this before we went travelling as I kept an exceptionally detailed log from day one. Below is an exact copy of the first page of that log.

My Travel Log

PETROL & TRAVEL COSTS

5/8 €50
7/8 €40
14/8 €50
16/8 €50
20/8 €50
21/8 Boat. Denmark – Norway, 2,350 DKT (€300)
22/8 To Foerland. 2 boats, 70kr, 150kr (€24), 2 tolls, 70kr, 160kr (€24)
25/8 To Geiranger. 280 NKR (€30)
23/8 €50
Got bored doing this! Just assume we spent a shitload on petrol and tolls and boats and autobahn.

The Cost

FLIGHTS/INSURANCE

<u>*Qantas. Amsterdam via London return, peak season.*</u>

Two adults	Bought on points
Two kids	€1,625
Family travel insurance for 12 months	€938
Total flights and insurance	**€2,563**

FRANKI THE MOTOR HOME

Fiat Frankia 2.5D
6/7 berth
1992, 125,000 kms

Upfront Costs

Purchase	€13,500
Registration	€600
Green card insurance (12 months)	€500
Fitting out	€600
Sheets, barbecue, chairs, table, cooking equipment, cutlery, electric heater	
Total	**€15,200**

Repairs and maintenance

Croatia	€1,000
Engine repairs and radiator/oil service	
Portugal	€220
New tyres	
Finland	€240
New water pump	

Bulgaria Glow plug	€50
Morocco Oil service	€50
Turkey Oil service, wipers, new lights, broken bumper	€180
Total	**€1,740**

Less Resale

| Net sale proceeds after storage costs and commission | €6,500 |
| **Total Franki the motor home net costs** | **€10,440** |

SPENDING MONEY ON THE ROAD

Fuel 42,000 kilometres 7 kilometres per litre at €1 per litre	€6,000
Arrival/departure hotel accommodation (3 nights)	€300
Accommodation Average of €18 per day for 283 days	€5,094
Free camping 82 days (incl. 6 weeks London)	Nil
General – groceries/wine/beer/ferries €90 per week	€4,680
Eating out, entertainment Average €35 per day	€12,775
Apartment Dubrovnik Two weeks	€1,100
Apartment Kraków Two nights	€110

Flights Madrid to London return	€480
Camper storage in Madrid €11 per day for 42 days	€462
Internet	€350
Telephones	€500
Various clothes, presents	€1,000
Total Spending Money	**€32,851**

Total Gross Trip Cost: €45,854

Currency	€euros	$AUD	£UK	$USD
Exchange Rate	1	1.6	.68	.82
Total Outlay	€45,854	$73,366	£31,180	$37,600
Per Person	€11,463	$18,341	£7,795	$9,400
Per Day	€126	$201	£85	$103

Total Net Trip Cost: €30,104

Adjusted costs after deductions from our personal circumstances.

Net income from our house rent $AUD600 per week for 42 weeks	$AUD25,200 (€15,750)

	€euros	$AUD	£UK	$USD
Exchange Rate	1	1.6	.68	.82
Total	€30,104	$48,166	£20,470	$24,685
Per Day	€82	$132	£56	$68

Note: Exchange rates based on the average conversions at the time of travel.

Summary: we should do it again sometime!

Thinking of going on your own adventure?

Let's not plan too much... it goes against the zing of just jumping. But I thought a few starter ideas might be helpful – and some space to jot down your own.

Camper/RV/Motor home

To buy or not to buy?
Three months is the magic number. If you are travelling for any less time, rent. Any more... look at buying.
Do your own numbers on the hire fee for the starship you want to explore in.

HOW MUCH DID IT COST?

The Must-Haves

I am not going to list nappy wipes and waterproof shoes and all that stuff. Technology is going to have to be your own call, although I strongly suggest that if you truly want to connect with each other, with the scent of flowers or the tune of a violinist, disconnect.

The comprehensive list of things we couldn't live without:

- iPod with speakers and thousands of songs
- The four-wheel-drive in-line collapsible double stroller
- A non-stick frypan
- Warm bedding
- Enough toilet chemicals to dissolve a dead horse in a dam
- Lots of books, toys, teddies and a pack of cards
- A laptop for movies and photos
- A digital camera
- Writing pads and pens
- A guide that has 50 basic words in every language: *Hello. Goodbye. How much? That's too expensive! Where is the toilet? Is this really animal meat?*

Five items I would specifically add:

- Two awesome tilt-back deckchairs
- A Europe GPS
- An e-reader
- Speedos, in case you want to swim in a public pool in France
- Peacock screech in a bottle (yet to be invented)

HOW MUCH DID IT COST?

HOW MUCH DID IT COST?

Travel Costs

There were two things that helped us keep the budget somewhat under control:

1. Making our own meals in camp. But then again, what is Europe without dining out and stuffing little faces with gelato? For us, lunch became a great experience: specials are available, carafes of wine are cheap, and the kids still have some zing in them that they don't flap around on the restaurant floor like beached catfish.

2. Free camping. The more free camps, the better financially, but there is a trade-off with small kids. In the enclosure of campsites, they can run around with gay abandon, as long as the playground has passed inspection. For this freedom, for them and us, we bush camped far less than we could have.

Use our costing to create your own 'budget'. Then add a bit for those uncontrollable splurges when the food is too good, the wine too smooth, and the museum too great to miss.

HOW MUCH DID IT COST?

HOW MUCH DID IT COST?

ACKNOWLEDGEMENTS

So many people came on this ride and helped me produce a book far beyond my own individual prowess. Firstly I must thank the stars of the show, my kids, Jaimie and Callum, whose presence constantly reminds me to keep living as though magic and miracle exists.

I thank my mother Nance and her friends at the Ballycara Retirement Village, whose unbridled joy in my scrawled travel letters over the years inspired all my writing. Maree and Paul, my sister and brother, have always added their laughter, advice and support. To my parents-in-law Esther and Rodney Johnson, their guest appearance on the road had a more inspirational impact on our family than they will ever know. I thank Christina Katic, lifetime family friend and writer; her guiding tips at various stages helped me chart the way through the story. I am also fortunate to have a host of friends, too many to name, who delivered unconditional encouragement when it was needed most.

To my literary agent Selwa Anthony, her advice, support and endorsement of the book will always be appreciated. I thank Abbie Headon at Summersdale Publishers; her instant enthusiasm for the story and subtle editing has given it a wonderful boost. It has also been a joy to work with

ACKNOWLEDGEMENTS

Robert Drew and Dean Chant at Summersdale. Finally, my deepest gratitude is to my wife and fellow writer, Mandy Johnson. To have her literary instincts on call was invaluable. But more so, she has been the only one, from start to finish, who constantly challenged, encouraged and believed in me. Quite simply, this book would not exist without her.

Have you enjoyed this book?
If so, why not write a review on your favourite website?

If you're interested in finding out more about our books,
find us on Facebook at **Summersdale Publishers** and
follow us on Twitter at **@Summersdale**.

Thanks very much for buying this Summersdale book.

www.summersdale.com

PRAISE FOR *ON THE ROAD... WITH KIDS*

Full of laughs but owes more to Eat Pray Love *than it does to* National Lampoon. *As they swerve from one kooky situation to another, amid all the fun and foibles of travel is an honest, heartfelt meditation on the meaning of modern life. A profound recalibration of priorities. A charming and life-affirming read.*

SYDNEY MORNING HERALD

A rollicking read that leaves you relieved to be safe at home.

COUNTRY LIFE

Hats off to a couple willing to share one chemical toilet with two kids and not want to kill each other. One to make harried parents everywhere stop and smell the roses.

SYDNEY DAILY TELEGRAPH

This is no A–Z for budding campers. This is a morality tale, a manual for life, an affirmation for involved parenting. The campervan is not merely a vehicle, but a metaphor for unrequited dreams, for seizing the day.

THE COURIER-MAIL

An unhurried journey across Europe in a rickety motor home gives a dad time to learn how family works.

SYDNEY SUN HERALD

A year-long European vacation. The escapist fantasy quickly became grounded in more basic demands. In between the many stresses on this nomadic adventure, John manages to reassess his priorities, 'noticing things I never would have when previously hurtling through life's daily activities'.

MELBOURNE SUNDAY AGE

The further they travelled from their old lives, the more they peeled back those artificial layers of personality that accumulate over years of career-building and responsibility. For Ahern, it was like a corporate snake shedding its skin.

BUSINESS REVIEW WEEKLY

You are going to be an inspiration to many people through the book – an example of how to live for real. And it made me laugh out loud.

CHRISTINA KATIC, PLAYWRIGHT OF *THE BLOOD THAT'S IN YOU* (BBC TV) AND *SICK* (GRAEAE THEATRE COMPANY)

With extraordinary honesty and a wonderfully wry and laconic sense of humour, Ahern takes us into the heart of life and out of all our comfort zones. Adventure after adventure he shows us just what we can be as family when we choose to let go the norm. I loved every page of this book, every failure, joy, surprise and success.

PETA-LYN FARWAGI, AUTHOR OF *THE LIFE BALANCE PROGRAMME, THE AUSTRALIAN TRAVELLER'S HANDBOOK,* AND *FULL OF BEANS*

ON THE
ROAD
...WITH KIDS

ONE FAMILY'S
LIFE-CHANGING GAP YEAR

JOHN AHERN

summersdale

ON THE ROAD… WITH KIDS

This edition published in 2016 by Summersdale Publishers Ltd

First published by Pan Macmillan Australia Pty Ltd in 2014

Copyright © John Ahern, 2014

Summersdale Publishers Ltd
46 West Street
Chichester
West Sussex
PO19 1RP
UK

www.summersdale.com

Printed and bound by CPI Group (UK) Ltd, Croydon, CR0 4YY

ISBN: 978-1-84953-800-8